BETWEEN
LOVE
&
SUBMISSION

A TUG OF LOVE

OKEY ONUZO

Between Love and Submission

Copyright © 2020, Okey Onuzo

ISBN: 978-1-880608-16-6

FIRST EDITION
Published by,
Life Link Worldwide Publishers,
175 Raymond Court Fayetteville GA.

For more information and book orders: amazon.com
Call:
Email address: okeyonuzo@yahoo.co.uk

TABLE OF CONTENTS

ACKNOWLEDGEMENTS

———— ◆◇◆ ————

All glory to God who gives us grace to express this treasure we carry in earthen vessels with the strength and power which the Holy Spirit supplies.

I must acknowledge my children for inspiring this book. Dilichi was at the forefront of pushing that a book that addresses love and submission is very much needed because many young couples are having unnecessary stress.

Dinachi felt that the narrative is very much one sided. So much is said about a woman's submission but not much is taught about her husband's love.

Chibundu and Kassim joined the discussion now and again and Chinaza, Uche, and Onu all lent their support. Mariam with whom I have lived over forty years of love and submission was encouraging from the sideline.

My book editor Nneka Okonkwo did a great job rearranging the chapters after the book was written.

Finally, I must thank God again that, in this book, Between Love and Submission, I have a follow-up to my earlier book on choice, engagement, courtship and wedding – You May Kiss the Bride.

PREFACE

———————— ◆◇◆ ————————

The experience of married life can range from living happily ever after, to the monster of irreconcilable differences. To those who lived happily after the wedding, sometimes they wonder how they managed to cross the bridge of integration to settle down to a relationship of love and peace. To those who had to face irreconcilable differences the wonder is always, "what went wrong? How did the promise of a great future together fizzle out into this present nightmare?" The Bible has two key words that determine outcome. The first is love and the second is submission. In an earlier work, *You May Kiss the Bride,* it is stated that there are three things we are in search of when choosing a life-partner: There is the *love of my life* – someone they are deeply attracted to. There is *the love for life* – someone who will be with them till the end of their journey together. The third is the *destiny partner* – someone with whom they will walk the path of God's will and so fulfill their destiny together. They envisage to be destiny helper to each other in many different ways. The question is, do those who succeed stumble at it or do we have principles that guide us through the tussle of integration to the bliss of harmony, love and peace? Between Love and Submission is about how to get through the tussle of integration and quickly settle down to a life of love, peace and harmony. Those beginning the journey of married life will find this book a great help in reducing the time spent in this tussle that goes with blending two persons from different backgrounds into a couple married for love and for life. Those already on the journey but sense that the relationship is not heading in the direction of love, peace and harmony may find principles here that can assist them to walk the path of a badly needed course correction. No matter where you are on the journey of life as a married couple, this book may serve to articulate what you did right for those who found love, joy and peace. For those on the road to irreconcilable differences, my prayer is that the Holy Spirit will show you what to do to turn the relationship around to the glory of God. And for those who have found their tussle endless with much unhappiness and misery, my prayer is that the Holy Spirit will help you see that there is a way to put an end to a life of endless tussle and settle down to love, joy, peace and harmony in your marriage.

Okey Onuzo

December 2020

INTRODUCTION

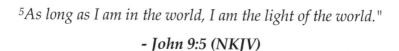

5As long as I am in the world, I am the light of the world."

- John 9:5 (NKJV)

One of the most powerful statements made by our dear Lord and Saviour Jesus Christ is recorded in John chapter 9, verse 5: "As long as I am in the world, I am the light of the world." Our Lord Jesus Christ came to be the Light of the world. In introducing Him in His Gospel, the Apostle John said in **John 1:4 (NKJV):** *4"In Him was life, and the life was the light of men."* The life that our Lord Jesus brought here was the light to drive away every darkness, evil, wickedness, and oppression that men and women had contrived in their dark minds, while it was controlled by darkness of evil.

The world that our Lord Jesus met when He arrived was full of evil, distortion and relegation of truth. It was full of oppression and injustice with much insensitivity in inter-human relationships that includes family. He came with knowledge and authority to set right many ideas and notions that were wrong. He came to lay the foundation of love in all relationships. First it must be a relationship between God and man where we must know that loving God means obedience and reverence. Then it must be a relationship of love between man and his fellow man where we must know that love is revealed through warm and kind thoughts with actions that speak louder of those virtues than words. Every area of life was impacted by His teachings and message of peace, kindness and love. He commissioned His disciples to go into the world and be light in a world of darkness and evil. He commissioned them to go and bring love to several traditionally strained and oppressive relationships in the world.

One sector of social relationship that was in total disarray in His society was marriage. Divorce was so easy for men. All they needed was a note given to the woman to say, you are free to go, with or without reason. The society outside the Jewish Church was even worse in their treatment of their women. In some societies, they were the property of their husbands to dispose of as they wished. In other societies they were neither to be seen nor heard from. Children fared even worse in the secular society of the time. A father had the power of life and death over his son and a son remained under the authority of his father until his father was dead even if he was seventy years and above. So long as his father was alive, he was under the authority of his father.

What the Apostle Paul wrote to the Galatian Christians was revolutionary: **Galatians 3:27-29 (NKJV):** *27"For as many of you as were baptized into Christ have put on Christ. 28There is neither Jew nor Greek, there is neither slave nor free, there is neither male nor female; for you are all one in Christ Jesus. 29 And if you are Christ's, then you are Abraham's seed, and heirs according to the promise."*

It must have been a 'Wow' statement to the ears of the women of his time who were accustomed to the oppressive norms of the day. That men and women are now equal in Christ with no separation and no distinction must have been music to their ears. It must have required deep conviction and great courage for the Jewish men who first preached the Gospel of Jesus Christ to defy the opinion of the day and raise the social level of women in their society.

I suppose Christian assemblies were the first taste of this equality before God. Whereas in the temple, the court of the women was completely separated from the court of the men to the extent that the women hardly saw any worship ritual in the temple, the Christian assemblies where men and women mix freely and women directly participate in the worship service was a huge leap. If early Christian Jews could take such a leap and defy culture and tradition, it is time for this generation of Christians to establish a home that is ruled by love and kindness to enable Christian homes shine the Light of Jesus in this world of darkness.

My prayer is that this generation will reveal the power of love in their families to fulfill God's original intent revealed in **Genesis 2:24 (NKJV)** [24]*"Therefore a man shall leave his father and mother and be joined to his wife, and they shall become one flesh."*

CHAPTER ONE

MUTUAL SUBMISSION IN THE HOME

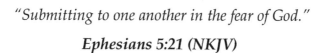

"Submitting to one another in the fear of God."
Ephesians 5:21 (NKJV)

*"Submit yourselves to one another because of
your reverence for Christ."*
Ephesians 5:21 (TEV)

The teaching on close family relationships begins with the admonition to mutual submission out of reverence for Christ. Two people made to become one can start with mutual submission. This Scripture reveals that submission is not oppressive and is not unidirectional. Instead, it is how members of the Body of Christ express their togetherness and their oneness in purpose and conduct. They are king and priest unto God created to bring God glory on earth in their relationships. When we learn mutual submission in Church, we practice it at home to build a union that glorifies God and His Christ in our lives.

From Practical Word Studies (PWS), we learn that; 'To submit' means to humble one's self; to obey; to offer; to succumb, to surrender, to relinquish. When this is mutual, it creates a powerful dynamic for peace and harmony in the home. This teaching may be against the couple's background culture, which is what often creates conflict. The Apostle who wrote this was a Jewish man and understood the impact on the culture.

We get no small help backing away from oppressive cultures from the statement, *out of reverence for Christ.* The authority directed through loyalty and reverence to Christ is the power that drives the change in attitude. Through a primary devotion to God and His Son, our obedience acquires the force to defy all cultural pressure and produce a relationship that is the admiration of our peers, who may prefer to toe the cultural line. Some of these cultural tweets are anecdotes. One says that a man cannot be seen or known to be listening to his wife. When we obey the Word of God, we may appear foolish to some of the people around us. But we see how through weakness, we are made strong in the LORD and empowered to be the shining light amid a crooked and perverse generation.

The Bible tells us how God uses these seeming weaknesses to confound those who are wise in their own eyes as revealed in **1 Corinthians 1:27-28 (NKJV):**

27 But God has chosen the foolish things of the world to put to shame the wise, and God has chosen the weak things of the world to put to shame the things which are mighty;

28 and the base things of the world and the things which are despised God has chosen, and the things which are not, to bring to nothing the things that are,

The practice of mutual submission may seem weak to a macho man accustomed to self-assertion and autocracy. But through submitting to one another out of reverence to Christ taught and practiced in Church, we learn to give and take at home, to build a home that glorifies God. Besides, God can evolve a family relationship that inspires others to love, peace, and harmony when we joyfully submit to each other in love.

A man who belongs to a Church group led by a woman can easily see how mutual submission in Church helps us understand and practice the same virtue at home. In our Church, we have had Sunday School Superintendents who were women. They led the Church Sunday School department creditably with great diligence and wisdom. If the husband of such a lady would follow his wife in Church but will not listen to her at home because she is his wife, the clause, out of reverence to Christ, will help him back away from the culture to embrace the truth as it is in Christ.

Sometimes, it takes a while to figure out where a spouse is coming from and what things are typical in their world. One spouse may come from a home where everyone washes their dishes after a meal for example. However, all you do in the other home is to leave the dirty dishes in the sink for some paid worker to come and clear. And now, there is no paid hand, and one spouse is still dropping dishes in the sink all the time for "angels" to do the washing even when their hands can work for the "angels."

The couple can discuss such a situation objectively; doing the dishes immediately after food will save the kitchen from cockroaches and reduce the labor in doing the dishes. When you leave them till later, they become an obvious chore. Mutual submission will involve either doing them if one has more time than the other, and they leave home later or getting to the meal earlier to accommodate the dishes. After one or two children have come, the mornings will require a lot more juggling to run smoothly.

Many little things like this cause friction to be dispensed with easily if there is love and mutual submission. Anyone who clings to gender defined roles may create a situation of stress where it should not exist. The Scriptures say that the two have become one, and they should labor together to build a haven of peace and rest for themselves and to the glory of God.

CHAPTER TWO

LEADERSHIP IN THE HOME THE HEAD
OF THE MAN IS CHRIST

———————— ◆◇◆ ————————

When the Scriptures say that the head of the man is Christ, it reveals that the man is to learn leadership from Christ. He is to lead his family in the same manner that Christ is leading him. So, to understand what that means, we have to look at our Lord Jesus' leadership style.

He called His disciples to be with Him

The Bible reveals that to raise a group of people who would follow in His footsteps, our Lord Jesus took them in as understudies in **Mark 3:14 (Passion NTPsa)**

"Afterward, Jesus went up on a mountainside and called to himself the men he wanted to be his close companions, so they went up the mountainside to join him. He appointed the Twelve, whom he named

apostles. *He wanted them to be continually at his side as his friends and so that he could send them out to preach and have authority to heal the sick and to cast out demons."*

The Apostle Paul stated the leadership style of understudies in **1 Corinthians 11:1 (NKJV):** "Imitate me, just as I also *imitate* Christ."

Our Lord Jesus Christ's leadership style is primarily designed to allow understudies to see how He does God's will on earth as it is done in heaven by precepts and by example. Repeatedly, He stated to their hearing: *"I came down from heaven to do the will of the Father who sent Me." (John 6:38, John 4:34)*

Lesson in Summary

The Bible records that our Lord's disciples were no different initially from any group following their leader anywhere today. They were ambitious, carnal, and exhibited the jealousy and rivalry seen in similar groups. What matters is that by the time our Lord Jesus was through with them, quite a few had gotten the truth that to lead is to follow Christ well enough to be the example to follow among men.

Luke 22:24-28 (NKJV)

"Now there was also a dispute among them, as to which of them should be considered the greatest.

"And He said to them, "The kings of the Gentiles exercise lordship over them, and those who exercise authority over them are called 'benefactors.'

"But not so among you; on the contrary, he who is greatest among you, let him be as the younger, and he who governs as he who serves.

"For who is greater, he who sits at the table, or he who serves? Is it not he who sits at the table? Yet I am among you as the One who serves.

"But you are those who have continued with Me in My trials."

Those who follow our Lord Jesus as Head

When we follow the Jesus model as leaders, we realize that leadership is about being the example to follow and not about telling others what to do. In being that example, the followers have the following characteristics:

- They understand and practice love and transparency (John 5:19-20)
- They understand and do the will of God with unqualified obedience (John 4:34)

- They practice leadership by example, not by precepts alone (John 13:12-17)
- They model virtues to inspire obedience and loyalty (Luke 22:27)
- They teach and model forgiveness (Luke 17:3)
- They teach and model humility and service in love (Luke 22:26)
- They understand that leadership is not in a vacuum but that we use our relationships to reveal the nature of Christ in us. (Luke 22:28)

The Model to Follow

The man's leadership model is revealed in two ways; First, there is the love between the Father and the Son. This love has full transparency that inspires unquestioning obedience. The Son sees and knows all that the Father is doing and is delighted to follow in the Father's footsteps. Notice that the Father's love and transparency are the driving forces behind the Son's inspired obedience in everything.

The second model is the self-sacrificing love of the Son for us revealed in **John 15:12-13 (NKJV):**

"This is My commandment, that you love one another as I have loved you. "Greater love has no one than this, than to lay down one's life for his friends.""

The love of the man must be modeled and patterned after the self-sacrificing love of Christ. Besides being self-sacrificing, it is also inspirational and is the standard for measuring our love. "As I have loved you" means to the measure and the same degree of My love for you.

Our Lord Jesus calls us to follow Him

I have noted over the years that anywhere you have a struggle for position in any group it is proof that they are carnal and are not cast in the mould of our Lord Jesus Christ. Those who pattern their leadership style after Christ our Lord know that in leading others, they are simply showing them how to follow Christ to do the will of God on earth in all things, as it is done in heaven. In our next chapter, we shall see how this applies to leadership at home.

CHAPTER THREE

LEADERSHIP AT HOME

—————— ◆◇◆ ——————

From the study of Genesis chapter 3, where this topic originated, this is an order of leadership and accountability. It places the responsibility of leading a family to do the will of God on earth as it is done in heaven, squarely on the shoulders of the man. And in doing this, he is to model his leadership style after the leadership style of our Lord and Saviour Jesus Christ.

When we look at Ephesians chapter 5 from verse 21 to Chapter 6:1-9, which deal with family relationships, we see that this is a part of a much broader discussion of spiritual life's practical dimensions. This discussion is what is called the out-workings of our salvation in **Philippians 2:12-16 (NKJV):**

12Therefore, my beloved, as you have always obeyed, not as in my presence only, but now much more in my absence, work out your own salvation with fear and trembling;

¹³for it is God who works in you both to will and to do for His good pleasure.

¹⁴Do all things without complaining and disputing,

¹⁵that you may become blameless and harmless, children of God without fault in the midst of a crooked and perverse generation, among whom you shine as lights in the world,

¹⁶ holding fast the word of life, so that I may rejoice in the day of Christ that I have not run in vain or laboured in vain.

To work out our salvation practically amid a perverse and crooked generation, we must shine as light in a world of darkness and show ways of love, service, and obedience that are far superior to what the world is practicing. There is every reason why we must not jump to Ephesians 5:21, while ignoring the rest of the discussion and teaching that started from Ephesians 4:17.

Learning the Way of Christ – The Old Way Versus the New Way

Ephesians 4:17-24 (NRSV)

¹⁷ Now this I affirm and insist on in the Lord: you must no longer live as the Gentiles live, in the futility of their minds.

¹⁸*They are darkened in their understanding, alienated from the life of God because of their ignorance and hardness of heart.*

¹⁹*They have lost all sensitivity and have abandoned themselves to licentiousness, greedy to practice every kind of impurity.*

²⁰*That is not the way you learned Christ!*

²¹*For surely you have heard about him and were taught in him, as truth is in Jesus.*

²²*You were taught to put away your former way of life, your old self, corrupt and deluded by its lusts,*

²³ *and to be renewed in the spirit of your minds,*

²⁴ *and to clothe yourselves with the new self, created according to the likeness of God in true righteousness and holiness.*

The task here is quite simple. A Christian couple must recognize that there is an old way of the world of unbelievers for conducting family relationships, and there is a new way.

The Old Way

Here are the things we learn about the old way:

- This is the way of unbelievers here called Gentiles.
- Their understanding is darkened or simply dark and laden with iniquity.
- They do not know the new Life of God through Christ.

- They have lost all sensitivity and have abandoned themselves to diverse lusts of the flesh, greed, and all manner of impurity.
- We are to put away our former way of life as unbelievers with all its lusts and corruptions, selfishness, and insensitivities.
- We are to clothe ourselves with a new mindset created in God's likeness and pursuing righteousness and holiness on the earth.

A Christian couple must know that we are to model Christ to our world. We are not just called to be husband and wife like every other person in the world but are to show the way for those around us to see Christ's life in a marriage setting. We are told in the Book of Romans that this is obligatory: **Romans 8:12-14 (NKJV)**

"Therefore, brethren, we are debtors--not to the flesh, to live according to the flesh. For if you live according to the flesh you will die; but if by the Spirit you put to death the deeds of the body, you will live. For as many as are led by the Spirit of God, these are sons of God."

The New Way

The first thing we note about this new way is that it is a learned way. The subject is Christ. We learn to live the life of Christ.

- The new way of Christ does not mix the old ways with the new way; rather, it discards all the old ways to embrace Christ's new life for married couples.
- It calls for a renewal of the mind, which means to change the way we are thinking about marriage relationships. We are to discard all our pre-conceived notions to embrace Christ and the new life He brought into the world.
- In this new way, we declare that the truth is in Christ. Therefore we are determined to learn and practice the new way of life in Christ, particularly its uniqueness as light in a world of darkness.

Learning the new way

We embrace the new way through a careful study of the Word of God.

Ephesians 4:25-32 (NRSV)

25So then, putting away falsehood, let all of us speak the truth to our neighbors, for we are members of one another.

²⁶*Be angry but do not sin; do not let the sun go down on your anger,* ²⁷*and do not make room for the devil.*

²⁸*Thieves must give up stealing; rather let them labor and work honestly with their own hands, so as to have something to share with the needy.*

²⁹*Let no evil talk come out of your mouths, but only what is useful for building up, as there is need, so that your words may give grace to those who hear.*

³⁰*And do not grieve the Holy Spirit of God, with which you were marked with a seal for the day of redemption.*

³¹*Put away from you all bitterness and wrath and anger and wrangling and slander, together with all malice,*

³²*and be kind to one another, tender-hearted, forgiving one another, as God in Christ has forgiven you.*

Here are the things the Christian couple should take into their relationship

- Put away falsehood and tell the truth to each other.
- Be angry but don't sin by postponing forgiveness and reconciliation. Be sure to reconcile before the day is over.
- Be sensitive to the pleasures and displeasures of the indwelling Holy Spirit. Each time we embark on the wrong way, He will stir our conscience to alert us that we are going in the wrong direction.

- Reject every element of theft, through corruption, whether at home or in the office.

- Weigh the words you speak to each other, and be sure it is seasoned with salt to edify or build-up and not hurt or put down. (Colossians 4:6)

- Do not entertain bitterness, anger, quarrels, and slander; neither hold grudge or malice.

- Habitually show kindness, forgiveness, and tender loving care.

The Christian Couple as Light

The first 12 verses of the fifth chapter of Ephesians is a continuation of the general principles of godly living for the Christian, which the young Christian couple needs to imbibe. **Ephesians 5:1-12 (NRSV)**

1 Therefore be imitators of God, as beloved children,

2and live in love, as Christ loved us and gave himself up for us, a fragrant offering and sacrifice to God.

3But fornication and impurity of any kind, or greed, must not even be mentioned among you, as is proper among saints.

4Entirely out of place is obscene, silly, and vulgar talk, but instead, let there be thanksgiving.

⁵Be sure of this, that no fornicator or impure person, or one who is greedy (that is, an idolater), has any inheritance in the kingdom of Christ and of God.

⁶Let no one deceive you with empty words, for because of these things the wrath of God comes on those who are disobedient.

⁷Therefore, do not be associated with them.

⁸For once you were darkness, but now in the Lord you are light. Live as children of light –

⁹for the fruit of the light is found in all that is good and right and true.

¹⁰Try to find out what is pleasing to the Lord.

¹¹Take no part in the unfruitful works of darkness but instead expose them.

¹²For it is shameful even to mention what such people do secretly;

Here are the lessons we have to imbibe:

Be imitators of God

Our God has revealed Himself in Christ Jesus, our Lord. When we look at the life our Lord Jesus Christ lived on earth, we can learn to imitate God on the earth. This tutelage embodies all the love, humility, and inspirational leadership, leadership by example, which our Lord Jesus revealed while He was here on earth.

Walking in Love

Live in love, and this love used here is *agape* or unconditional love. As Christian couples, we are to walk daily in self-sacrificing, unconditional love. The emphasis is on self-sacrificing love. *"For God so loved the world that He gave us His only begotten Son."* Christ so loved us that He sacrificed His life to save us." We have Scriptures that speak to us about the love of God and the love of Christ.

Romans 5:7-8 (CSB Bible)

[7]For rarely will someone die for a just person — though for a good person perhaps someone might even dare to die. [8]But God proves his own love for us in that while we were still sinners, Christ died for us.

We learn from this that as people who imitate God, we don't only show love when our spouse is good and does things that please us. We show love consistently because God gave us His best gift while we were His enemies. This attitude is how we learn to show love always and unconditionally, whether we are upset or happy. When we can show love this way, we have joy in our souls because we have risen from our earthiness to emulate deity's nobility. Now we know that there is divinity or God-nature inside us as human beings waiting to be released by the act of our will. The new nature of Christ within us has acquired a controlling voice over the things we say and do.

The love of Christ is compelling. The Apostle Paul discovered this in **2 Corinthians 5:14-15 (CSB Bible):**

"For the love of Christ compels us, since we have reached this conclusion, that one died for all, and therefore all died. And he died for all so that those who live should no longer live for themselves, but for the one who died for them and was raised."

This knowledge has practical implications daily. I have to love my spouse as if it was Christ showing them love. The reason is that I should have died for my sins, but Christ died for me, releasing me to go into my world and live His life rather than my own. This mindset conquers ego, particularly when a couple is inclined to strife or compete against each other rather than cooperate. If we stop to say to ourselves, *"Wait a moment, 'I am dead.'* Christ is now the one to respond. So, from what the Bible has revealed to me about Christ, how would He react in this situation?" This approach is how the compelling power of Christ's love works in our relationships as Christians to transform us and manifest the new life of Christ planted in us by the Holy Spirit.

Stay away from immorality

We are to stay away from immorality and to keep the marriage bed undefiled by sin as taught us in **Hebrews 13:4 (NRSV):**

"Let marriage be held in honor by all, and let the marriage bed be kept undefiled; for God will judge fornicators and adulterers."

We shall deal a lot more with this when we look at conjugal love later. Suffice it to say that the Bible teaches that a married couple owes it to each other to meet their emotional needs as revealed in **1 Corinthians 7:1-7 (CSB Bible):**

[1]Now in response to the matters you wrote about: "It is good for a man not to have sexual relations with a woman."

[2]But because sexual immorality is so common, each man should have sexual relations with his own wife, and each woman should have sexual relations with her own husband.

[3]A husband should fulfill his marital duty to his wife, and likewise a wife to her husband.

[4]A wife does not have the right over her own body, but her husband does. In the same way, a husband does not have the right over his own body, but his wife does.

[5]Do not deprive one another — except when you agree for a time, to devote yourselves to prayer. Then come together again; otherwise, Satan may tempt you because of your lack of self-control.

⁶I say this as a concession, not as a command.

⁷I wish that all people were as I am. But each has his own gift from God, one person has this gift, another has that.

Stay Away from Covetousness and Greed

Stay away from covetousness and greed, for this is a form of idolatry. Our Lord Jesus taught in Matthew 6:24 that we could either serve God or mammon, not God and mammon. When thoughts began to come to me as the pioneer of private dialysis in Nigeria; I recall thinking of expanding to other cities in Nigeria from my base in Lagos. We even toyed with the idea of getting a small aircraft to attend to the dire emergencies that might arise. When I took the option to the LORD in prayer, I could sense a chuckle from heaven. The reason was that running just one location caused my Blood Pressure to rise from its usual 120/70-80 max to 170/120 on one occasion. That reading was an eye-opener of what could happen to us when we raise our stress level. In the end, one centre was all I did, and my Blood Pressure is down to reasonable levels of 130/80-85 and thanks to God, I did not sustain any end-organ damage while it lasted. Indeed, the LORD our God knows our way through life's wilderness, and it is in our best interest to follow His leading in all things. Only God can see the future now and give us the counsel we need to make life-changing and life-threatening decisions correctly with all things considered. If I had persisted in going that multiple expansion route, undoubtedly, the cost to my health would have been high, not to talk about the price I would have had to pay in the stability of my home and relationships with wife and children. I discovered that the promise to supply my needs proved true without risking my life and health unduly: **Philippians 4:19-20 (CSB Bible):**

[19]*And my God will supply all your needs according to his riches in glory in Christ Jesus.*
[20]*Now to our God and Father be glory forever and ever. Amen.*

Shine as Light in your world

A Christian couple must always remember that they are to shine as Light in the world by manifesting the life of our Lord Jesus Christ. This calling in Christ is the purpose that controls and drives our determination to get it right more often than not. This mindset is particularly vital after children begin to arrive. They must learn that dad and mum maintain the highest ethical and moral standards in their conduct. For a child to grow up believing that being corrupt or dishonest is normal is a monumental tragedy. We had a law in our home that says, "if something is wrong, it is wrong. It does not matter who did it, whether they are old or young and whether they are parents or children. It is the same rule for all. Such a practice ensures that children are not confused about right and wrong.

Stay with the will and delight of God Almighty always.

To always find out what is pleasing to the LORD, our God is to enter into the inner circle of God through obedience born of love and loyalty. When we have people around us as human beings, who desire to please us always, we know they will be close to us. This disposition is more so with God, who can spot genuine love and loyalty. Besides, because God is love personified, we can always be sure that His revealed will for us is in our best interest. I recall having a musing with God when I was in private practice after my National Youth Service stint. I lay on the bed discussing many issues with the Lord. I was still single and getting ready to wed. I recall saying to the LORD that evening: "LORD, if I end up not doing postgraduate, I am not sure I would be happy." He did not respond, but within four months of that musing, my early private practice period was brought to a screeching halt one month after my wedding. It took nine months for me to come to terms with the fact that God answered my musing and redirected me to do postgraduate studies in internal medicine. All the doors in private practice shut in my face with such finality. When I enrolled for postgraduate studies in internal medicine, the late Professor Deji Femi-Pearse welcomed me with open arms and graciously enrolled me in December for a program that had started in June or July at the Lagos University Teaching Hospital. I had so much favour, and I knew it was all divinely orchestrated.

Stay Away from Secret Sins

There is no room for secret sins because there is nothing secret before the Almighty God. This truth is foundational Christianity. We need the Holy Spirit to keep watch over our souls so that we escape every snare on our path of life. The couple should always remember what the psalmist said: that God has perfect and complete knowledge of us in **Psalm 139:3-7 (NRSV):**

3 "*You search out my path and my lying down, and are acquainted with all my ways. 4 Even before a word is on my tongue, O LORD, you know it completely. 5You hem me in, behind and before, and lay your hand upon me. 6Such knowledge is too wonderful for me; it is so high that I cannot attain it. 7 Where can I go from your spirit? Or where can I flee from your presence?*"

Now we know why there is no escape from the gaze of Almighty God for any human being on this earth. The reason is in **Proverbs 20:27 (NRSV):**

²⁷"*The human spirit is the lamp of the LORD, searching every inmost part.*"

The human spirit is the animating or life-giving spirit. If it leaves the body, the body will become lifeless. But God gave us of His Spirit at creation (Genesis 2:7). That spirit keeps us alive, and when it leaves us, we die. But here is an insight into the work He does within us revealed in **1 Corinthians 2:11 (CSB Bible):**

"*For who knows a person's thoughts except his spirit within him? In the same way, no one knows the thoughts of God except the Spirit of God.*"

The spirit in man knows all our thoughts, and that is why we cannot hide our thoughts from God. The spirit in us is from God. We can see why we can keep this Scripture in our memory: **Hebrews 4:13 (CSB Bible):** ¹³"*No creature is hidden from him, but all things are naked and exposed to the eyes of him to whom we must give an account.*"

Therefore, the couple must know that there can be no secret before God and no hiding place from Him. Anyone who thinks that they can hide whatever they are doing from God is at the very best deluded. Those who introduce deception into their family relationship will sooner than later pay a heavy price at the discovery.

Redeem the Time

If ever there was a Scripture whose direct relevance has come in time, it is this one:

Ephesians 5:15-16 (NKJV)

[15]*See then that you walk circumspectly, not as fools but as wise,* [16]*redeeming the time, because the days are evil.*

To redeem the time is to exercise ourselves in godliness at every juncture of life and resist every attempt by the world to lure us into dissipation. This challenge calls for much thought and caution in making our choices and planning our actions, knowing that we do not have all the time to do God's will on the earth. For this reason, every time available to us must be rigorously deployed and maximally applied in the pursuit of godliness, which serves our benefit in time and eternity. When a couple does this, they will be pulling their weight and effort in the same direction for the desired result of peace and harmony in their home. Two people in pursuit of godliness and the goal of the divine will, through obedience to God's Word, will lapse into a depth of harmony that is unimaginable.

Understand what the will of the Lord is

A couple that takes time to understand the LORD's will in every situation that confronts them, will discover the path to love, harmony, and peace. For example, suppose they have a misunderstanding: in that case, they will pause to figure out individually how the Word of God directs them to react, or they will hear the voice of the Holy Spirit in their hearts urging them to the path of peace, reconciliation, and friendship. The will of the LORD is for unity, love, amity, and harmony. The will of the LORD is for peace and love through forgiveness and self-sacrifice. To understand what the will of the LORD is in every situation is the gold standard.

Be Filled with the Holy Spirit not with wine

Intoxicants, when used in excess, diminish responsibility. The Ephesians worship the god of wine, Bacchus, and it was customary in their worship ceremonies to get intoxicated with wine. The Apostle said to these new Christians, "*Do not join in the intoxicating orgies that go on in these pagan ceremonies. Instead, be filled with the Holy Spirit.*" When we are filled with the Holy

Spirit, He is allowed to produce His nine-fold fruit in us and through us to nourish our marriage relationship. The fruit of the Holy Spirit is the bedrock of happiness in marriage – love, joy, peace, patience, goodness, kindness, faithfulness, meekness, and self-control. Whatever situation or challenge that arises within marriage, the Holy Spirit within us will manifest the appropriate fruit to counter it.

Giving thanks always

Praise and thanksgiving are powerful, tried, and tested weapons of warfare to counter challenges and retain a godly atmosphere in the home.

Ephesians 5:20 (NKJV)

"Giving thanks always for all things to God the Father in the name of our Lord Jesus Christ,"

The journey of faith for a couple in Christ cuts across times and seasons when praise and thanksgiving will carry us across many troubled rivers on the road of life. One of the things I learned about giving thanks for all things is that no matter how bad something appears to be, it could still be worse. So, we know to give thanks to the LORD for His mercy that shielded us from a worse outcome. Then we rise to give Him thanks and praise for what He will yet do to glorify His name in our situation. Understandably this may be tough to do, but those who have done it know that it is mighty indeed in repositioning us to continue to trust and hope in God no matter the situation. Many wonderful miracles of divine intervention under challenging circumstances await families that rise to praise the LORD God Almighty in trying conditions, and testimonies will abound.

Besides, there is a bonding power when two people go through adversity together by faith. They learn to pray together and to trust God together for survival and sustenance. They come away from trouble with a deeper and a better understanding that two are better than one. They are stronger together, united in love and faith, able to draw down God's help and favor in challenging situations.

My wife and I experienced this between December 1978 and September 1979 when I lost my private practice job and was waiting to go into postgraduate training. Although we were barely a month married, the crisis bonded us together as we supported each other through the nine months with my locum earnings and her National Youth Service Corp wages. We learned to trust God together and to hope in God for a brighter future. After over forty years, we are alive to testify that it pays to trust the LORD and obey His Word.

CHAPTER FOUR

BETWEEN LOVE AND SUBMISSION

——————— ◆◇◆ ———————

22 Wives, submit to your own husbands, as to the Lord.
25 Husbands, love your wives, just as Christ also loved the church
and gave Himself for her,
Ephesians 5:22&25 (NKJV)

In the above two verses of Scripture: verse 22 that says, wives submit to your own husbands and verse 25, that says, husbands love your wives, we have the driving principles of a peaceful and harmonious family relationship. A man and his wife can live happily ever after if they are able to follow these stated principles in both spirit and letter.

Love before Submission or Submission before Love?

But the question is often asked, which comes first? Is it love before submission or submission before love? There is the suggestion that because submission is in verse 22 and love is in verse 25, submission should come before love. That is very simplistic in my opinion. We could take it to other things in the Bible that we are commanded to do. Here is the order of the second part of the ten commandments:

Exodus 20:13-17 (NKJV)

¹³ "*You shall not murder.*

¹⁴ "*You shall not commit adultery.*

¹⁵"*You shall not steal.*

¹⁶"*You shall not bear false witness against your neighbor.*

¹⁷"*You shall not covet your neighbor's house; you shall not covet your neighbor's wife, nor his male servant, nor his female servant, nor his ox, nor his donkey, nor anything that is your neighbor's.*"

Can we say by any stretch of imagination that this order is an order of significance? What is more realistic is to look at each of the commandments and what they relate to and whether they are before or after. Pray for grace to stay away from all and every evil.

The Husbands Charge

The way to determine which is first is to look at what each of them says. Husbands are to love their wives as Christ loved the

Church. Once you accept that husbands are to love their wives as Christ loved the Church, then you have accepted that husband's love must come before the wife's submission for that is the way Christ loves the Church. The love of Christ was first before the Church's submission. The Bible actually states this in **2 Corinthians 5:14-15 (NKJV):**

14For the love of Christ compels us, because we judge thus: that if One died for all, then all died; 15 and He died for all, that those who live should live no longer for themselves, but for Him who died for them and rose again.

It is the love of Christ that is compelling and inspiring the Church's submission. Several years ago, a preacher said to us that the way to deepen our individual loyalty to Christ is to go in our meditation to the Cross of Calvary and there re-live the events of His passion. As we behold the blood drop from His side and spell out the four-letter word, L O V E, we will come away with a deeper sense of obligation and loyalty.

Sometime in the nineteen eighties, I preached an Easter message titled: "CAN YOU SEE HIM?" As I and the audience went to Calvary and followed the nailing, the hanging, the forgiveness of his tormentors and the pain and suffering of His agony, there was hardly a dry eye in the congregation including mine. That

Okey Onuzo

day has stayed with me and in my heart to continually inspire my dedication to Him and my commitment to His service. It was not just the Apostle Paul that was compelled and inspired by His love and sacrifice but many in every generation have gone to Calvary to be moved by the love and the sacrifice that bought us our judicial pardon revealed in these two Scriptures:

Isaiah 53:6 (NKJV)

6 *All we like sheep have gone astray; We have turned, every one, to his own way; And the LORD has laid on Him the iniquity of us all.*

2 Corinthians 5:20-21 (NKJV)

20 *Now then, we are ambassadors for Christ, as though God were pleading through us: we implore you on Christ's behalf, be reconciled to God.*
21 *For He made Him who knew no sin to be sin for us, that we might become the righteousness of God in Him.*

The Church's Submission – A Response

It is quite clear that man's loyalty to God is a response to God's love. The Bible states it clearly in **1 John 4:9-10 (NLT2):**
9 *God showed how much He loved us by sending his one and only Son into the world so that we might have eternal life through Him.*

42

¹⁰This is real love – not that we loved God, but that He loved us and sent His Son as a sacrifice to take away our sins.

Love came first

We did not know God until Christ came as the messenger and epitome of God's love as revealed in that most famous Scripture **– John 3:16 (NKJV):**

¹⁶For God so loved the world that He gave His only begotten Son, that whoever believes in Him should not perish but have everlasting life.

When love goes first, it inspires and empowers submission. It is important to understand the great power of the love that goes first. Anyone who fails to respond to the initiative of love stands condemned as the Scriptures say:

John 3:17-19 (NKJV)

¹⁷For God did not send His Son into the world to condemn the world, but that the world through Him might be saved.

¹⁸He who believes in Him is not condemned; but he who does not believe is condemned already, because he has not believed in the name of the only begotten Son of God.

¹⁹And this is the condemnation, that the light has come into the world, and men loved darkness rather than light, because their deeds were evil.

The Power of Self-Sacrificing Love

It is important to understand the power of self-sacrificing love, not just to inspire but to be light in the world of selfishness and insensitivity. The love of Christ is the Light of the world. It is the Light to give light to everyone in the world as revealed in **John 1:4-5 (NKJV):**

[4] *In Him was life, and the life was the light of men.*
[5] *And the light shines in the darkness, and the darkness did not comprehend it.*

The Christian is the light of the world. A man and his wife become this light when the husband loves his wife and his love inspires his wife and children to an unqualified love and submission to his leadership.

Could submission come before love?

To suggest that a wife's submission must precede her husband's love is to put the cart before the horse. What that will mean is that it is our submission to Christ that inspired His love for us. Nothing could be farther from the truth. It is the love of Christ that is the driving force that continues to inspire our submission. In fact, it is the fact that we trust in His love and the faithfulness of His love and care that we go to every length to obey and serve Him.

God's order of responsibility, accountability and leadership

What we see in Genesis chapter 3 is an order of responsibility, accountability and leadership as revealed in **Genesis 3:9-13 (NKJV):**

9 Then the LORD God called to Adam and said to him, "Where are you?"

10 So he said, "I heard Your voice in the garden, and I was afraid because I was naked; and I hid myself."

11And He said, "Who told you that you were naked? Have you eaten from the tree of which I commanded you that you should not eat?"

12Then the man said, "The woman whom You gave to be with me, she gave me of the tree, and I ate."

13And the LORD God said to the woman, "What is this you have done?" The woman said, "The serpent deceived me, and I ate."

Having determined what the problem was, the LORD God Almighty set this order for responsibility, accountability and leadership: **Genesis 3:16 (NKJV):**

16To the woman He said: "I will greatly multiply your sorrow and your conception; In pain you shall bring forth children; Your desire shall be for your husband, And he shall rule over you."

The Hebrew says that the longing of the woman shall be channeled or directed to her husband who should be the governor or ruler of their home. This is an order of leadership, responsibility and accountability. The ruler of the home is responsible and accountable to God for the spiritual, physical and emotional welfare of the home. In the pursuit of his great task, his family is to submit to his authority in the home to make his task easier. It is for this reason that the Bible puts love before submission. As the love of Christ inspires His bride the Church, so should the love of a man continually inspire his wife.

The King that Rules by Love

Some years ago, I preached a message on the above subject – THE KING THAT RULES BY LOVE. The kings of this world rule by force deploying and employing all manner of force and coercion. But the King we serve rules us by love. He does not force us into submission rather He loves us into submission.

John 15:12-15 (NKJV):

¹² This is My commandment, that you love one another as I have loved you.

¹³ Greater love has no one than this, than to lay down one's life for his friends.

¹⁴You are My friends if you do whatever I command you.

¹⁵ No longer do I call you servants, for a servant does not know what his master is doing; but I have called you friends, for all things that I heard from My Father I have made known to you.

We must know that if our love fails to inspire submission and obedience, then we must seek to yield to the Holy Spirit so He would love through us with the love of Christ.

The Power of the Love of Christ

What we learn from the love of Christ is that it elevates the Church to be by His side and lifts us to share His nature.

- The love of Christ makes us to become one with Himself as revealed in **John 14:20-21 (NKJV):**
  ²⁰At that day you will know that I am in My Father, and you in Me, and I in you.

²¹He who has My commandments and keeps them, it is he who loves Me. And he who loves Me will be loved by My Father, and I will love him and manifest Myself to him."

- The love of Christ causes us to share in His honour and glory. So, it lifts us up and never puts us down as revealed in **Ephesians 2:4-6 (NKJV):**

  ⁴But God, who is rich in mercy, because of His great love with which He loved us,

  ⁵even when we were dead in trespasses, made us alive together with Christ (by grace you have been saved),

  ⁶and raised us up together, and made us sit together in the heavenly places in Christ Jesus,

Wives, Submit to Your Own Husband

I recall how the Lord led me to lay the ground rules for submission in our home in the early days of our marriage. I said to my wife in many words: "I do not want to know what you think: I do not want to know what I think either. But if the Holy Spirit is speaking to you on any matter in hand, that is what I want to know." The reason I said that is that my primary responsibility as the head of the family is to lead the household to do the will of God in any and every matter or situation.

Submission to me is actually to Christ who is my head. So long as I am leading my family to do the will of God the ground beneath my authority is as solid as a rock. God did not hand over the family leadership to the man so the family will do the man's will. To the contrary, the man is to lead the entire family to do the will of God. That was the problem in the Garden of Eden. Nobody was in charge of doing the will of God on earth in the family. If Adam had been in charge, Eve would have had to ask him if it was okay to give the forbidden fruit a bite. Adam, knowing that he would have some serious explaining to do when God arrives might have had a second thought and thus humanity might have been saved the tragedy of the fall of man. All speculation, for there is nothing to suggest that Adam would not have committed the same error had the devil approached him first.

A wife must therefore be prayerful so that if she senses the husband is going in the wrong direction, she will point it out to him and pray that God will help him see it. It is in the manner in which she points it out that reveals her submission. It must be courteous. I had an opportunity to counsel with a young couple years ago. The problem was that the lady would sense that the husband was headed in the wrong direction on an occasion. She would point it out to him but he would refuse to turn. When he hits a rock or faces a disappointment or failure, she will position herself to say, "I told you so." By the time they came to me she claims it had happened numerous times without number.

At that point, I asked her if it was possible for him to hit a rock after such a counsel and she would not say to him, "but I told you so." She told me outright that it was not possible because she had told him so and he would not listen. I advised her to stop saying "but I told you so," to enable him start listening to her. Nobody likes to hear, "but I told you so." It is like rubbing salt into the wound of failure so that it will really hurt. Fortunately, they worked it out in time and are now the counsellors of many still trying to figure out the path to peace and harmony in a Christian home.

Submission is the path of the wise woman who builds her home and manages to gather the household to follow her in living under the authority of her husband who is the head of their household. Several times while growing up I saw my mother attend to visitors to our home when my father was away on his many trips to conferences for regional school supervisors of Anglican schools. My mother would listen to them carefully and say afterwards: "You will have to come back because my husband is not at home." I heard that phrase, "My husband is not at home" countless times. It was not that my mother was incapable of making those decisions; what she wanted to convey to the visitor is that there is a head of household and the decision cannot be made without him. That was long before the days of telephone and now mobile phones.

There is one particular incident that I remember very vividly. I had my paternal aunt's son living with us in Jos. His father who was the Chief of our town sent someone to come from the East to Jos to bring him for Christmas but he did not tell my father. When my father got to the village for the annual December Church and community meetings and was told of it, he was furious and went to Orlu to send a telegram to my mother that the boy must not travel. Everything was set for them to go to the train station on their trip south, when the telegram arrived at about 7 pm. The train was leaving an hour or so later. My mother calmly but firmly told the man that he would have to go away without the boy. That lesson spoke volumes to me about how women can let everyone around them know that they are submitted to their husband's authority.

Now my mother could easily have said: "But it is their child. They are at liberty to collect him anytime they liked." It is harsh to say no and dash the boy's hope of a travel, which we loved so much as children. That would have been disastrous for my father's authority over his household. Not once did I notice my mother defy my father openly. I am sure they had their disagreements now and again in private but it was never for the ears and eyes of outsiders.

As the LORD commanded Moses

Moses described the exodus of the Hebrews from slavery as an act of God in **Deuteronomy 4:32-35 (NKJV):**

32"For ask now concerning the days that are past, which were before you, since the day that God created man on the earth, and ask from one end of heaven to the other, whether any great thing like this has happened, or anything like it has been heard.

33 Did any people ever hear the voice of God speaking out of the midst of the fire, as you have heard, and live?

34 Or did God ever try to go and take for Himself a nation from the midst of another nation, by trials, by signs, by wonders, by war, by a mighty hand and an outstretched arm, and by great terrors, according to all that the LORD your God did for you in Egypt before your eyes?

35 To you it was shown, that you might know that the LORD Himself is God; there is none other besides Him.

But for this feat to be possible Israel had to do everything as the LORD commanded Moses. Now, if we go through the Bible, we will note over five thousand five hundred instances of this phrase: "as the LORD commanded Moses." Without that submission, the Exodus of the Hebrews from Egypt would not have been possible.

The Wife who submits as the LORD commands her husband

It is important to note the power of following God by following the husband who is following God. It has such awesome power that it almost always guarantees divine favour. Permit me to share one or two personal testimonies.

We travelled to the USA for my one-year fellowship program as a family in 1982. It was God Almighty who said to go with all the family. Other colleagues used to go alone and leave their families in Nigeria. To be able to finance that, we had to sell one of our cars and we felt obliged to give out the other. When we came back a year later, we had no transportation but got a gift from the hospital where my wife worked, to stay mobile and do school runs.

I told the LORD in prayer that I needed to buy a Volvo, some durable car that will last us years. To cut a long story short, my wife said we could not afford it. We argued back and forth and while we argued I was unable to mobilize the funds. One day it dawned on me as I prayed that favour is lacking because of our lack of agreement. So, I pleaded with her to just agree with me and not to worry about the money. Three days after we agreed in prayer, the car was parked in front of our house, a new Volvo with just 4000 miles that belonged to the Swedish ambassador. It was an eye-opener. There was favour all around from the bank to the ambassador. The great thing is that we never missed a payment until the loan was liquidated.

The next crucial experience was when my first daughter was going to the United Kingdom for A levels. When my wife and my daughter first broached the subject with me, I told them pointedly that she will not go even if we had all the money unless I knew that the LORD had approved it. And for a very long time I heard nothing one way or the other. So, the matter was left on the shelf. I recall my daughter coming periodically to say to me, "Daddy, have you heard from the LORD now?" I would say, "No." and she would say, "I am praying. I would say, "Good!"

I was travelling in the USA when I heard God say to me, "Let her go." I came home and left a note where they could see it. It was excitement all around when they discovered the note.

The point that was made clear to me was that the LORD has to approve it since the payment is about funds of the future and we cannot see the future now. And to the glory of God, we went through that phase of our lives as a family without a major hitch. At no time were the children out of school as a result of funds.

A husband leads his family to follow Christ

What makes submission easy for a woman and her children is this demonstrated knowledge that the head of their home is leading them to follow where God is leading the family. You could then see this as a common dialogue:

"We are going to Benin from Lagos for the weekend," the husband says.

'Have you prayed? Is that what the Lord is saying?"

"Yes, I believe so."

"Ok. I will pray too because I want to go to Enugu not Benin."

Now suppose the man goes back to God and hears the Spirit say: "Nothing special about Benin. If she prefers to go to Enugu, then go to Enugu. It is neither here nor there." This is where an issue may arise. The man may say: "But LORD I have said Benin, so it has to be Benin. I cannot change my mind." Then the woman returns to say, "Well, I really prefer Enugu to Benin but if you have a special thing with Benin, it's okay." Then the man retorts: "Actually, I don't have any special thing in Benin. So, if you prefer Enugu, let's go there."

This is the kind of example that shows us how mutual submission works hand in glove with a wife's submission. Now take another travel opportunity for the family. This time around, the man asks his wife if she has a preference for their destination. "Yes, I have," she says. "Jos, the Hill Station hotel in Jos. I visited there as a child many years ago."

The man goes off to God in prayer. Surprisingly, there is a big 'no' that came as a stop sign to his vision. When he communicated that to his wife, she was not pleased. She became suspicious that the husband may have found a way to turn down her proposals by saying the Lord did not approve. She made a lot of fuss and would not accept to go anywhere else. It was either Jos or nowhere else. But fortunately, the day before they were to leave for Jos, there was news of riots in the city and they had to cancel their trip. It began to dawn on her after that, that the husband may be hearing from God after all. There is a Scripture that supports this kind of development in **Psalm 144:1-2 (NKJV):**

[1] Blessed be the LORD my Rock, Who trains my hands for war, and my fingers for battle –

[2]My lovingkindness and my fortress, My high tower and my deliverer, My shield and the One in whom I take refuge, Who subdues my people under me.

When a man is following the LORD, the Holy Spirit will show him how to handle the disagreements and conflicts that occur at home particularly during the phase of integration. In the end, the LORD will help his family to submit to him by making them see that he is following the LORD and not his own whims and caprices. That is why King David said that God is the one who subdues my people under me. He makes the people see that the hand of the LORD is upon David for the good of all. The same way, a wife may come to realize that the husband is not opinionated but is striving to walk like our Lord Jesus Christ did as He revealed in **John 5:19 (NKJV):**

¹⁹*Then Jesus answered and said to them, "Most assuredly, I say to you, the Son can do nothing of Himself, but what He sees the Father do; for whatever He does, the Son also does in like manner."*

There is a learning curve in this for a couple. Initially they may have a lot of stress trying to sort out the challenge of two walking together in agreement as one. With time things improve when the virtues needed to walk in harmony are in place as we shall see later.

The constraints of following the Lord

When husband and wife are Christians filled with the Holy Spirit, we can suppose that they have the potential for communion with the Holy Spirit. Following the Lord when two people can hear the Holy Spirit's communion should make matters relatively easier. Making decisions would be a matter of who is hearing God clearly. And when there is a disagreement each person should have the grace to set aside passions and listen to the counsel of the Holy Spirit. This is what should happen when two people are one but one of them is walking ahead and leading the way.

The Natural, the Carnal and the Spiritual

The Bible reveals that the natural man does not receive the things of the Spirit of God. He cannot understand these spiritual principles that govern family relationship because they are spiritual in origin.

1 Corinthians 2:14 (NKJV):

14 But the natural man does not receive the things of the Spirit of God, for they are foolishness to him; nor can he know them, because they are spiritually discerned.

The carnal man may have received the grace of God that brings salvation but has not learnt to deny ungodliness and worldly lusts (Titus 2:11). As a result, he has a behavioural pattern that is no different from that of the unbeliever.

1 Corinthians 3:1-4 (NKJV):

1And I, brethren, could not speak to you as to spiritual people but as to carnal, as to babes in Christ.
2I fed you with milk and not with solid food; for until now you were not able to receive it, and even now you are still not able;
3for you are still carnal. For where there are envy, strife, and divisions among you, are you not carnal and behaving like mere men?

⁴For when one says, "I am of Paul," and another, "I am of Apollos," are you not carnal?

The spiritual man on the other hand has the mind of Christ and has a clear sense of right and wrong in all situations or will recognize and accept the right if he sees or knows it.

1 Corinthians 2:15-16 (NKJV):

¹⁵But he who is spiritual judges all things, yet he himself is rightly judged by no one.
¹⁶For "who has known the mind of the LORD that he may instruct Him?" But we have the mind of Christ.

And now we shall proceed to study these two passages of Scripture in greater detail.

CHAPTER FIVE

WIVES SUBMIT TO YOUR
OWN HUSBANDS

———————— ◆◇◆ ————————

As many of you as were baptized into Christ have clothed yourselves with Christ. There is no longer Jew or Greek, there is no longer slave or free, there is no longer male and female; for all of you are one in Christ Jesus.

Galatians 3:27-28 (NRSV)

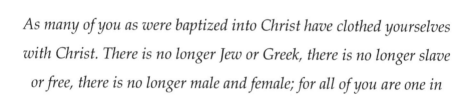e must go to the text to be able to appreciate this subject fully. Here is the passage of Scripture: **Ephesians 5:22-24 (NRSV):**

²²*Wives, be subject to your husbands as you are to the Lord.*
²³*For the husband is the head of the wife just as Christ is the head of the church, the body of which He is the Saviour.*
²⁴*Just as the church is subject to Christ, so also wives ought to be, in everything, to their husbands.*

Here are the things we need to be fully obedient to the Word of God.

- Wives are to be subject to their husbands in the same way that they are subject to the Lord Jesus Christ. We must note that a wife is not subject to husbands. A wife is to submit to her husband, just one husband. No other person should have such authority over a woman other than her husband.

- The husband is the head of his wife in the same way that Christ is the head of the Church, which He sacrificed His life to save.

- This submission has a pattern. The way a woman submits to Christ is by volition, as an act of devotion, which is in acknowledgement of Christ's self-sacrificing love.

- In the same way, a woman is to be subject to her husband, who is nourishing her with his self-sacrificing love.

- For this reason, it is generally said that submission is inspired in women by the self-sacrificing love of their husbands. Even when it is initially inspired by obedience to the Word of God, it should be sustained by self-sacrificing love.

- This is the same way that we all are inspired to love and submission to Christ because of His self-sacrificing love towards us.

- The love of Christ is a compelling love (2nd Corinthians 5:14). It compels obedience and submission volitionally by its sheer depth and quality, particularly by the sensitivity of His care and all His provisions.

- When a wife is nourished daily by a self-sacrificing love, the wife is expected to respond with a willing submission to her husband's authority and leadership in the home.

- Submission is never demanded. To demand submission is to admit failure of leadership. A successful leader never states the obvious.

- A man is the head of his wife, but men and women are equal before God, particularly as saved souls in Christ. Husband and wife are baptized in the name of the Father, the Son, and the Holy Spirit. Husband and wife are baptized into Christ and have become members of His body.

- Besides, husband and wife receive the same Holy Spirit as Comforter, Counsellor, and Guide. This is why they are called to walk together in love to fulfill the will of

God for their lives as a family unit. Above all, they are to show the beauty and the glory of Christ to the world.

- It is for this reason that the Bible states in **Galatians 3:27-28 (NRSV):** *27As many of you as were baptized into Christ have clothed yourselves with Christ. 28 There is no longer Jew or Greek, there is no longer slave or free, there is no longer male and female; for all of you are one in Christ Jesus.*

What Submission is Not

It is important to state that submission is not suppression or oppression; neither is it domination. It is neither demanded nor forced with any form of coercion. A young lady about to wed stopped by my office for medical consultation. Our banter drifted to pre-marriage counselling. She told me that she and her fiancé were attending some classes in their local Church. That made me curious, and I wanted to hear what they were being taught. Here is what she said they were taught about submission.

"The officiating teacher stood up and sat down on the table instead of sitting behind it on a chair. He then asked one of the young ladies to come and squat under the table. He told the intending couples that a man sits on top of his wife the same way he is sitting on the table and the young lady is squatting under. Nothing could be farther from the truth. This kind of teaching creates confusion in young people's hearts and minds going into marriage. Those who may not have experienced true family love and unity where husband and wife complement each other actively are confused. We must stress that a wife's submission to her husband is always in response to her husband's self-sacrificing love.

Let me here repeat that submission is not oppression, nor is it suppression. Submission in the home is about leadership and the order of accountability and responsibility. A man is directly accountable to God for his wife and children's well-being. Through their submission, his wife leading their children is to make it easy for the man to fulfill the calling to lead their home in a godly manner. Through self-sacrificing love, he is to raise a well-nourished family, fed with a love that is patient and kind, a love that is not proud or boastful, and a forgiving love which does not keep a record of wrongs. This love is unconditional, and so it is the initiative that drives the family cohesion. Those who oppress or suppress their wives have no support whatsoever in the Word of God, as we shall see when we look at the man who loves his wife the way Christ loves the Church, His bride. But let's look from the perspective of early Christians.

Saint Chrysostom on Ephesians 5:22-25

"Have you noted the measure of obedience? Pay attention to love's high standard. If you take the premise that your wife should submit to you, as the Church submits to Christ, then you should also take the same kind of careful, sacrificial thought for her that Christ takes for the Church. Even if you must offer your own life for her, you must not refuse. Even if you must undergo countless struggles on her behalf and have all kinds of things to endure and suffer, you must not refuse. Even if you suffer all this, you have still done not as much as Christ has for the Church. For you are already married when you act this way, whereas Christ is acting for one who has rejected and hated him. So just as He, when she was rejecting, hating, spurning and nagging Him, brought her to trust Him by his great solicitude, not by threatening, lording it over her or intimidating her or anything like that, so must you also act toward your wife. Even if you see her looking down on you, nagging and despising you, you will be able to win her over with your great love and affection for her." (ACC for Ancient Christian Commentary on Scripture.)

What submission is:

With this in mind, let us proceed to study the wife's submission in detail.

- She should honour and respect her husband and submit to his leadership and authority within and outside the home. A lady told me some of the ways she practices this in her home. She relishes serving her husband at the dinner table. She will rise to dish out his food at the table and if he wanted another helping, she will rise to dish it as well. Once she had a friend join them at dinner. After grace, she rose to dish out her husband's portion before dishing out her own. Her friend simply stared at her in amazement. When her husband finished his portion, he said he needed another helping. As she rose to serve him again, her friend could not take it anymore. She told her to sit down because according to her she was spoiling her husband. She just laughed it off and continued with the exercise. Then she said her friend swore never to bring her own husband to their house for dinner before he will learn something "bad."

- There was this other story of a lady lawyer who used to courtesy to serve her husband. On one occasion when she had to give a drink to her husband in the presence of some of her friends, she curtsied as usual and that evoked a rowdy response from her friends: "What is this? Please get up. Don't you know you are a lawyer?" She simply told them that she likes to honour her husband.

- Most young people will feel embarrassed by such public displays that are tied to the local culture. Growing up in the Igbo culture here in Nigeria, my mother showed great honour and respect for my father but it is not in our culture for a wife to kneel to serve her husband. I remember a story told us by one of our leaders in Foursquare Nigeria. He and his wife were on a visit to the USA. Each time they shared a buffet meal in public with other ministers, he would sit down and his wife would go to bring his food. This would be customary here in Nigeria and no one would think anything of it. However, many of the ministers thought it was an anomaly. They observed it once, twice and may be the third time, they approached his wife and asked: "What is wrong with your husband? Is he sick? Can't he come for his food himself?" That was when it dawned on him that in the culture where they were, what he was doing was considered oppressive. He advised his wife never to serve him again in a public buffet. He would come for his food himself.

- Most women who honour their husbands in this way do so of their own volition. Women who do not do it this way also respect and honour their husbands in several other ways. For example, it was my mother's delight to put my father's stuff together each time he was to travel. And he never crosschecked to see that everything was there. He trusted her judgment in all such matters. Every time she cooks, she will ensure that my father gets the first portion. She drilled us on that repeatedly. Even when my father was not at home, his food must be dished and preserved for when he returned. Everyone was taught by word and example that my father was the head of the home. Often in family conversation we all learn to shut up when my father is talking. How often have I heard her or someone say: "Shut up, papa is talking!"

- Some would say that today's families are much closer than when we were growing up because children of today talk more but must do so respectfully. What is important for many couples to know is that times have changed and are continuously changing. It does not invalidate the nuances of honour and respect. But they should always be volitional for that is the bedrock of our relationship with Christ.

- A woman should inspire their children and all the household to acknowledge and accept her husband's leadership and authority in the home.

- Although there is no strict gender defined roles but the wife should take charge of organizing the home especially the feeding and care of the family. Her husband should follow her closely behind helping with whatever he can to fill the gaps. Like one lady put it to me: "I am the one who makes sure that everyone is taken care of. I am the home manager."

I have heard some women say that when their husbands enter their kitchen, they get in the way. So, they ask them to please stay away until they are done. This is particularly so for those who grew up in a home where their father never entered the kitchen. But in today's world where good and reliable domestic helps are expensive or hard to find, working as a team to manage the home is the best way forward. Yes, it is good for the woman to lead the way in organizing the home and for the man to follow so that they can work as a loving team.

I recall once when my parents visited our home with a little boy they adopted. It was after we had our first child. My mother assigned my father the duty of giving the boy his bath. I watched my father do this and saw how unused to such tasks he was. I did not offer to help him. Growing up at home my father never neared such chores because there were always several hands to undertake such tasks. But he was in his early seventies then and was probably doing such a chore for the first time or for the first time in several decades. But I was glad to see him rise to do it as part of his contribution to looking after the boy. This underscores the teaching on mutual submission in **Ephesians 5:21 (NRSV):**

[21]Be subject to one another out of reverence for Christ.

We will defer the area of decision making and allied matters in the home till later.

CHAPTER SIX

HUSBANDS, LOVE YOUR WIVES

In the same way, husbands should love their wives as they do their own bodies. He who loves his wife loves himself.
-Ephesians 5:28 (NRSV)

We must look at the Scripture in detail to get the true sense of the Word of God.

A Husband's Love for his Wife

We begin by looking at the text that details how a man should love his wife.

Ephesians 5:25-32 (NRSV)

^{25}*Husbands, love your wives, just as Christ loved the Church and gave himself up for her,*
^{26}*in order to make her holy by cleansing her with the washing of water by the word,*

27so as to present the Church to himself in splendor, without a spot or wrinkle or anything of the kind – yes, so that she may be holy and without blemish.

28In the same way, husbands should love their wives as they do their own bodies. He who loves his wife loves himself.

29For no one ever hates his own body, but he nourishes and tenderly cares for it, just as Christ does for the Church,

30because we are members of his body.

31"For this reason a man will leave his father and mother and be joined to his wife, and the two will become one flesh."

32This is a great mystery, and I am applying it to Christ and the Church.

BETWEEN LOVE AND SUBMISSION

We stated it categorically that the driving force in the family relationship is the husband's love. Husbands are to love their wives like Christ loves His Church:

Husbands love their wives like Christ – They take the Initiative

There is a lot more content to a husband's love in this passage of Scripture.

A husband's love is self-sacrificing

Ephesians 5:25 says: *"Husbands, love your wives, just as Christ loved the Church and gave himself up for her."*

This is a self-sacrificing love. It is a love that goes all out to do the highest good to his wife and does not do her any evil. We need to look for help at the Scriptures that reveal the love of Christ. **Romans 5:6-8 (NRSV):**

⁶*"For while we were still weak, at the right time, Christ died for the ungodly. ⁷ Indeed, rarely will anyone die for a righteous person – though perhaps for a good person someone might actually dare to die. 8 But God proves his love for us in that while we still were sinners Christ died for us."*

Other Scriptures teach that God took the initiative in Christ to love us as revealed in **1 John 4:9-10 (NRSV):**

⁹*"God's love was revealed among us in this way: God sent his only Son into the world so that we might live through Him. ¹⁰In this is love, not that we loved God but that He loved us and sent His Son to be the atoning sacrifice for our sins."*

So, we see clearly that the initiative belongs to the husband. He drives his entire family with his self-sacrificing love and devotion, inspiring and nourishing their devotion and loyalty to him.

Husband's Love is Unconditional

This is seen in the Greek Word used for this love: Husbands, *agapeo* your wives. The moment we parallel a husband's love with the love of Christ, we see why it is unconditional love. But what exactly does this mean?

- Unconditional love is a patient and forgiving love – it keeps no record of wrongs
- Unconditional love is constant and consistent because it does not depend on what the beneficiary does or does not do.
- Unconditional love is an act of the will. It is a choice. A man loves his wife. A man chooses to love his wife. A man has also decided to love his wife no matter what she does or does not do.
- Unconditional love inspires submission and loyalty, just as the love of Christ compels us.

Husband's Love is a Singular Love

A husband is to love his wife. He is not to share his love for his wife with other women. In the same way that a wife's submission is to her husband only, so a husband's love is for his wife only. Therefore, a man shall leave father and mother to be joined to his wife that the two may become one, naked or transparent and not ashamed or embarrassed. A man has no apologies for being one with his wife in every sense of the word.

Husband's love is a Nourishing love

Ephesians 5:26: *"In order to make her holy by cleansing her with the washing of water by the word,"*

A husband's love is to be spiritually nourishing to his wife. By modeling loyalty to Christ as the head, he inspires his wife to love and serve the Lord Jesus with all her heart. As they study the Word of God together, he leads in obedience to God and His Word, the way our Lord Jesus Christ loved and obeyed the Father: **John 14:31 (NRSV):**

[31]*"But I do as the Father has commanded me, so that the world may know that I love the Father. Rise, let us be on our way."*

This may not be as simple as it sounds because sowing seeds of repentance, forgiveness, and restoration may prove tough to do except with the abundance of God's grace. But when we spiritually nourish, we shine as light in a world of darkness and become a priceless jewel in our families to both wives and children.

A husband's love is a covering love

Ephesians 5:27: *"So as to present the Church to Himself in splendour, without a spot or wrinkle or anything of the kind – yes, so that she may be holy and without blemish."*

Part of this spiritual nourishment is that the wife has no spot or wrinkle in her character, just like Christ covers the Church. The implication of this is that whatever faults his wife has are to be covered by the husband's love not exposed by him. This covering is through forgiveness, patience, and understanding. As he sows these seeds into the life of his wife, he reaps a harvest of affection and submission. The preacher told the story of a couple who love to entertain guests. What many did not know was that the husband was the "professional chef." When the guests are at table, they heap compliments on the wife on her exquisite cuisine. The wife will accept it all, and the husband will smile along cheerfully. A gentleman suggested that his wife should stop over and learn her recipes. To which they both laughed and grinned some more without volunteering any information.

There was this other gentleman who took pleasure in buying dresses that fit his wife. He would spend hours in the shop, often asking ladies to help model a dress for him so he could see how it fits, many of whom obliged him. One day, he was cornered by a grandmother in a public space who wanted to know where his wife procured all her smart suits. He grinned and parried the question without volunteering any information. Our Lord Jesus covers our faults before the Father and, through the communion of the Holy Spirit, makes us look good to the world around us. And by this, we appear blameless and unblameable before God and are delightful before the world. This is the nature of a husband's love for his wife. It is patterned after the love of Christ. It is designed to cover her completely so that no fault of hers is exposed.

A Husband's Love is a Caring Love

We see this in **Ephesians 5:28**: *"In the same way, husbands should love their wives as they do their own bodies. He who loves his wife loves himself."*

A husband's love for his wife is to nourish the wife so that she is well aware of his love and care. He is to care for his wife as he cares for himself. This will involve a lot of hard work. The preacher told the story of a couple who were well bonded and quite close with warm affection. When someone wanted to know what it was due to, he was quick to credit the Holy Spirit that taught him that to love is to serve. "We serve those we love." The Holy Spirit revealed this to me in **John 13:12-17 (NKJV):**

12 So when He had washed their feet, taken His garments, and sat down again, He said to them, "Do you know what I have done to you?

13 You call me Teacher and Lord, and you say well, for so I am.

14 If I then, your Lord and Teacher, have washed your feet, you also ought to wash one another's feet.

15 For I have given you an example, that you should do as I have done to you.

16 Most assuredly, I say to you, a servant is not greater than his master; nor is he who is sent greater than he who sent him.

17 If you know these things, blessed are you if you do them.

In Christ, we learn to serve those we love without lectures but as leading examples of Christ's love. A man who loves his wife will step up to help at home with every manner of work needed to keep the house going. Some families can afford domestic managers who handle most of the chores. But it is important to note that a couple should not leave their children's care entirely to trained managers. Children should bond with their parents growing up, and this takes place in those early years of life.

A Husband's Love is Unyielding

Ephesians 5:31: *"For this reason a man will leave his father and mother and be joined to his wife, and the two will become one flesh."*

This is the love that never fails and which never breaks. It is that three-fold cord that is not easily broken because it is held together by the Holy Spirit's quickening power. When a couple is bonded in Christ, they have the inner strength to love as revealed in us by the Holy Spirit. As the Scriptures reveal, the Holy Spirit strengthens us with might in our human spirit so that we have the inner energy to walk in love in all situations. This is what it means to be rooted and grounded in love as revealed in **Ephesians 3:16-19 (NKJV):**

[16]that He would grant you, according to the riches of His glory, to be strengthened with might through His Spirit in the inner man, [17]that Christ may dwell in your hearts through faith; that you, being rooted and grounded in love, [18]may be able to comprehend with all the saints what is the width and length and depth and height-- [19]to know the love of Christ which passes knowledge; that you may be filled with all the fullness of God.

It is important to note that nobody can do all of these things in their strength. But the man who loves his wife and prays for grace to love her will discover a capacity beyond natural ability given him by the Holy Spirit.

A Husband's Love is Requited Love

Nowhere is this best illustrated as in **Ephesians 5:33 (AMP):**

[33]*"However, let each man of you [without exception] love his wife as [being in a sense] his very own self; and let the wife see that she respects and reverences her husband [that she notices him, regards him, honors him, prefers him, venerates, and esteems him; and that she defers to him, praises him, and loves and admires him exceedingly]."*

When a man loves his wife in the many ways stated above by the Word of God, his wife is to respond in these unique affectionate ways that nourish him and their relationship. It is the eternal law of sowing and reaping. But we must admit here that it is not always as cut and dried as this. Sometimes a man may sow and sow, and the harvest is withheld possibly due to insensitivity and carnality. On the other hand, a woman may also sow and sow to inspire the husband to an understanding of Bible-based love, but would wait a while to awaken Christian responses from him. To those who sow in hope in obedience to God and His Word, we have great encouragement from **Psalm 126:5-6 (NKJV):**

*⁵"Those who sow in tears shall reap in joy. ⁶He who continually goes forth weeping, bearing seed for sowing, shall doubtless come again with rejoicing, bringing his sheaves **with him**."*

This Scripture is a call for perseverance in following the path prescribed for us through the Word of God. It will bear fruit in due season, which maybe sooner or later.

Spiritual Maturity

Our response to genuine love or submission is a reflection of our state or level of spiritual maturity. When a wife submits to her husband, and he takes her for granted, it reflects the state of his spiritual maturity. The converse is also true. When a husband loves his wife with Christ-like love, and she takes him for granted, it reflects the state or level of her spiritual maturity. We say this without equivocation because of what the Bible says in **Romans 8:5-9 (TEV):**

⁵Those who live as their human nature tells them to, have their minds controlled by what human nature wants. Those who live as the Spirit tells them to, have their minds controlled by what the Spirit wants. ⁶To be controlled by human nature results in death; to be controlled by the Spirit results in life and peace.

⁷And so people become enemies of God when they are controlled by their human nature; for they do not obey God's law, and in fact they cannot obey it.

⁸Those who obey their human nature cannot please God.

⁹But you do not live as your human nature tells you to; instead, you live as the Spirit tells you to – if, in fact, God's Spirit lives in you. Whoever does not have the Spirit of Christ does not belong to him.

If both spouses are genuinely born again, sooner than later, the Holy Spirit will be able to reach them to toe the line of the way of the Spirit in their relationship.

The Husband Leading the way in Child Upbringing

The children are not left out in this God's order for the family as revealed in **Ephesians 6:1-4 (NKJV):**

¹Children, obey your parents in the Lord, for this is right.

²"Honor your father and mother," which is the first commandment with promise:

³ "that it may be well with you, and you may live long on the earth."

⁴And you, fathers, do not provoke your children to wrath but bring them up in the training and admonition of the Lord. (bold emphasis – mine)

Let us note the principles stated here for a couple to follow.

- Children are to obey their parents in the Lord. It is essential to secure this obedience with love and trust. A parent should convey to a child that his/her word is his/her bond. Parents should not deceive or confuse their children with falsehood.

- A parent should always act in honor by not doing what he/she had told the child is wrong to do. Whatever is wrong is wrong for children and adults too.

- Children are susceptible to partiality and injustice. Parents must do their best to avoid these, so they don't confuse their children.

- Children are believers in a sense. They will believe whatever you tell them until they see otherwise.

- Fathers are encouraged not to provoke their children by their insensitivity, oppression, and unnecessary punishment, particularly those out of proportion to the offense.

It takes the Holy Spirit to guide parents in the upbringing of their children. Every child is different, and the Holy Spirit knows each child and teaches parents how to take care of their wards.

Domestic workers are staff, not servants.

It is vital to note this. There is no place for verbal and physical abuse. There is no room for treating them with condescension. They should join the family prayers and study the Bible with the family. They learn godly character and behaviour through corporate meditation in the Word of God.

CHAPTER SEVEN

UNDERSTANDING GODLINESS

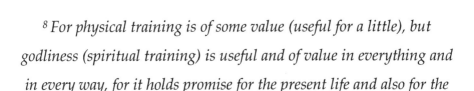

⁸ For physical training is of some value (useful for a little), but godliness (spiritual training) is useful and of value in everything and in every way, for it holds promise for the present life and also for the life which is to come.

- 1 Timothy 4:8 (AMP)

Godliness is profitable, valuable, and useful in everything and in every way. It has benefits in the life we live now: It also has benefits in the life we shall live in eternity. This statement is one of those statements on marble. A couple that desires to have and to hold with love, joy, and abundant happiness will need to understand and practice godliness in every sector of their lives. The pursuit of godliness will position and empower them to find love and joy in their union.

What is Godliness?

For this, we need to consult others.

"By godliness, we are to understand everything that the Christian religion either promises or prescribes: It is the life of God in the soul of man, and the glory of God as the object and end of that life."

(Adam Clarke's Commentary)

According to Saint Augustine: "'Godliness, which is the true worship of God, is profitable to all things,' 'Since it deflects or blunts the troubles of this life and leads to that other life, our salvation, where we shall suffer no evil and enjoy the supreme and everlasting good.'" (ACC)

Philipps Brooks said of godliness: "The great purpose of life — the shaping of character by the truth." (BEC)

"'Godliness' is just a clipped word. It was originally "Godlikeness," and it is so rendered in some older English translations. Godliness is genuine piety. That is its real meaning."

(H.A. Ironside Expository Commentary)

Godliness recognizes God Almighty for its source and law. Those who exercise themselves in godliness seek more of the reality of God, who is infinite love and wisdom, and more of His greatness and power in their lives.

If a couple is to have and to hold with love and joy, their emphasis on spiritual exercise must outstrip their focus on physical exercise. This spiritual exercise is the life of godliness as revealed in 1 Timothy 4:7 (AMP): *"But refuse and avoid irreverent legends (profane and impure and godless fictions, mere grandmothers' tales) and silly myths, and express your disapproval of them. Train yourself toward godliness (piety), [keeping yourself spiritually fit]."*

Use every opportunity of your life, particularly your marriage relationship, to get a spiritual exercise in godliness. Godliness is Godlikeness, as has been suggested above. When we exercise ourselves in godliness, therefore, we use every opportunity to inject one fruit of the Holy Spirit or the other into our lives. There is always room in marriage to practice love, joy, peace, patience, goodness, kindness, faithfulness, meekness, and self-control. When we deploy these virtues, we discover, for example, that it is not everything you see that you talk about; it is not everything you hear that should make you react. Quite a few, you must patiently correct without criticism. It is not everything that someone says that is upsetting that should upset you. You should have practiced forgiveness and have acquired a fresh dose of the love that covers a multitude of sins.

The place where we practice godliness is the soul where resides, our will, thought, and emotions. Every life opportunity can find its drill in our soul, causing us to imbibe one divine nature or the other. These virtues include but are not limited to the documented nine-fold fruit of the Holy Spirit.

CHAPTER EIGHT

EXERCISING YOURSELVES IN GODLINESS

Iron sharpens iron, and one person sharpens the wits of another.
Proverbs 27:17 (NRSV)

If a Christian couple is to have and to hold in love and joy until death or rapture separates them, it is inevitable that they will sharpen each other in their pursuit of godliness. They are not called to live out their selfish and individualistic natures within marriage, but they are to assist each other to manifest the divine nature that has been planted in them at salvation.

The Divine Assignment

Every married couple must take **Genesis 2:24** as a divine assignment. It is not just a statement to be read at weddings but a lifelong assignment to show that we are acquiring the divine nature through the exercise of godliness.

24Therefore a man leaves his father and his mother and clings to his wife, and they become one flesh. **(NRSV)**

Notice that we are taught that the Father, the Son or the Living Word and the Holy Spirit are one. When God created the man and his wife, He told them to go and achieve the same unity in the model of the Father, the Son and the Holy Spirit. This assignment is made possible by the fact that there is divinity within humanity. In other words, the nature of God is within us. We are to allow this God-nature to develop and manifest the unity that exists in God between the Father, the Son and the Holy Spirit in that unique relationship between a man and his wife.

This is the process whereby iron sharpens iron. We work to bring out the best in each other, so that after a while we notice that marriage has made each of us a better person evolving daily in the image and nature of Christ that we received at salvation according to **2 Peter 1:3-4 (NRSV):**

3His divine power has given us everything needed for life and godliness, through the knowledge of him who called us by his own glory and goodness.

4 Thus he has given us, through these things, his precious and very great promises, so that through them you may escape from the corruption that is in the world because of lust, and may become participants of the divine nature.

Adding Virtue to Each Other

To exercise ourselves in godliness, we must add virtue to the nature of Christ that we received at salvation. We grow to become more like Christ by adding virtue to our lives as revealed in **2 Peter 1:5-9 (NRSV):**

5 For this very reason, you must make every effort to support your faith with goodness, and goodness with knowledge, 6 and knowledge with self-control, and self-control with endurance, and endurance with godliness, 7 and godliness with mutual affection, and mutual affection with love. 8For if these things are yours and are increasing among you, they keep you from being ineffective and unfruitful in the knowledge of our Lord Jesus Christ. 9For anyone who lacks these things is nearsighted and blind, and is forgetful of the cleansing of past sins.

We must recognize that when we add virtue to our lives, it is tested daily in our marriage. If we add patience and endurance to our lives, iron will sharpen iron in the course of our interaction as a couple. My patience will be worked out in my relationship with my spouse. If I add kindness and goodness to my life, it will show up as kindness and goodness to my spouse. If I add humility and self-control to my life, it will be tested and proved in my relationship with my spouse.

Nobody adds virtue in a vacuum. Every virtue that we add must be tested and proved in the crucible of our family life. My journey to manifest the nature and character of Christ through my life, is nurtured, tested and polished in my family relationship.

CHAPTER NINE

GROWING THE GOD NATURE
THROUGH LOVE

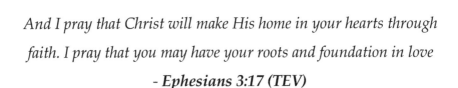

And I pray that Christ will make His home in your hearts through
faith. I pray that you may have your roots and foundation in love
*- **Ephesians 3:17 (TEV)***

ultivating endless love for each other in our
relationship is a no mean task. The Bible tells us that
it requires the infusion of spiritual energy as revealed
in this passage of which the above Scripture is a part: **Ephesians
3:16-19 (TEV)**

"I ask God from the wealth of his glory to give you power through his
Spirit to be strong in your inner selves,

"and I pray that Christ will make his home in your hearts through
faith. I pray that you may have your roots and foundation in love,

"so that you, together with all God's people, may have the power to
understand how broad and long, how high and deep, is Christ's love.

"Yes, may you come to know his love – although it can never be fully known – and so be completely filled with the very nature of God."

Notice the first prayer request in verse 16: It is for strength in the inner man infused by the Holy Spirit of God. But what exactly does this mean? The first thing we need to know is that we need strength to love. Love has challenges, and that is why we need to be strong to show an all-weather love. This strength is infused into our human spirit by the Spirit of God. The purpose is so that the spirit in us will have the energy to dominate our will, reorder our thoughts and our feelings with the Word of God. As an example, suppose as a couple, we left home for work in the morning. And we promised to each purchase stuff for the home because where they are sold is on our way. We come back and discover that one of us forgot totally. That led to dashed expectations. And without warning, a misunderstanding has already begun to brew.

"But what was on your mind that you forgot what I asked you to get?" one spouse asks with obvious disappointment.
"What do you mean by that? How could that be the only thing on my mind in a whole day? How could you be so rude?"
And in the middle of this kind of exchange, the Holy Spirit will nudge the one who forgot: "Just apologize."

And willingly or unwillingly, the offending party says to the offended party, "I am sorry. Trust me; it won't happen again."

And from heaven, this Scripture comes floating into the heart of the offended party: **Ephesians 4:31-32 (TEV)**

"Get rid of all bitterness, passion, and anger. No more shouting or insults, no more hateful feelings of any sort. Instead, be kind and tender-hearted to one another, and forgive one another, as God has forgiven you through Christ."

Growing Love in the Family

We receive much help from the Greeks in the understanding of family love. They have four words that describe family love.

The first is *Storge*. This word stands for **parental love for their children.**

Next is *Phileo*. This word stands for the warm affection between friends. It describes a relationship where sacrifices are made with joy, and nothing is a big deal at any time. In *phileo,* there is great warmth and passion.

Next is *Eros*. This word stands for conjugal love or the love between a man and a woman.

The fourth is *Agape*. This word stands for unconditional love. It is called the God kind of love because it is unconditional, as revealed in **Romans 5:7-8 (TEV)**:

"It is a difficult thing for someone to die for a righteous person. It may even be that someone might dare to die for a good person. But God has shown us how much he loves us – it was while we were still sinners that Christ died for us!"

Agape is love by choice, an act of the will. When we choose to love, we love unconditionally no matter what they do or do not do.

In growing love in the family, a couple needs to understand these four different kinds of love because they help us in no small way to love in the Christian home. And as we have seen in the study of the family relationship and order as revealed in Ephesians chapter 5 and part of chapter 6, these four different aspects of family love are needed for cohesion and harmony.

Love has Content and is Practical

It is important to note that horizontal love has content. It has its verbal expression, but it has content as well. This is stated for us in **1 Corinthians 13:4-8 (TEV)**:

"Love is patient and kind; it is not jealous or conceited or proud;

"love is not ill-mannered or selfish or irritable; love does not keep a record of wrongs;

"love is not happy with evil, but is happy with the truth.

"Love never gives up; and its faith, hope, and patience never fail.

"Love is eternal. There are inspired messages, but they are temporary; there are gifts of speaking in strange tongues, but they will cease; there is knowledge, but it will pass.

It is for this reason that we are counseled to be practical in our expression of love in **1 John 3:16-18 (TEV):**

"This is how we know what love is: Christ gave his life for us. We too, then, ought to give our lives for others! If we are rich and see others in need, yet close our hearts against them, how can we claim that we love God? My children, our love should not be just words and talk; it must be true love, which shows itself in action."

The Love of Christ Serves Others

Our Lord and Saviour Jesus Christ taught us to serve those we love. He demonstrated this very clearly in John chapter 13, when He laid aside His dress, took water, and washed the feet of His disciples. We must note what He said after that exercise in **John 13:12-17 (TEV):**

"After Jesus had washed their feet, he put his outer garment back on and returned to his place at the table. "Do you understand what I have just done to you?" he asked.

"You call me Teacher and Lord, and it is right that you do so, because that is what I am.

"I, your Lord and Teacher, have just washed your feet. You, then, should wash one another's feet.

"I have set an example for you, so that you will do just what I have done for you.

"I am telling you the truth: no slaves are greater than their master, and no messengers are greater than the one who sent them.

"Now that you know this truth, how happy you will be if you put it into practice!"

When He finished the exercise, He explained why He demonstrated service to others as the true expression of our love. He taught the disciples to learn happiness and joy that can only come to those who serve others in love. It was after this that He gave them His new commandment in **John 13:34-35 (TEV):**

"And now I give you a new commandment: love one another. As I have loved you, so you must love one another. If you have love for one another, then everyone will know that you are my disciples."

As disciples of our Lord Jesus Christ, we show our love humbly and practically the same way He showed it to us. When a couple decides to show love to each other the way our Lord Jesus showed it, they build a home where joy and laughter dominate the relationship because of humility and the love that serves others.

Growing the God nature

We must note that growing in love has an objective, which is to love like God and to show each other that we know God through our love as revealed in **1 John 4:7-8 (TEV)**:

"Dear friends, let us love one another, because love comes from God. Whoever loves is a child of God and knows God. Whoever does not love does not know God, for God is love."

The word used for love here is *agape,* the unconditional love. We show this in the family to each other. There is a practical understanding of this love. When we show unconditional love, we seek and do *the highest good to the person we love and never do them evil.* Here is the amplified rendering of **Romans 13:10 (TEV):**

"If you love others, you will never do them wrong; to love, then, is to obey the whole Law."

We never do wrong premeditatedly to those we love; instead, we do them the highest good possible. This way of love is how we grow the God-nature in us.

Strength to Love through Faith

It is the Holy Spirit that imparts the energy to love consistently, as we saw earlier from Ephesians 3:16. It is also the Holy Spirit that releases this God kind of love in our hearts as revealed in **Romans 5:5 (TEV):**

"This hope does not disappoint us, for God has poured out his love into our hearts by means of the Holy Spirit, who is God's gift to us."

We are indefatigable in our love because that love is given to and sustained in us by the Holy Spirit given us as Christians. We receive this love and the energy to express it by faith from the Holy Spirit. When we face challenges in our love relationship, we must know that there is strength to love through the power of the Holy Spirit. We receive this by faith through prayer. It works according to what our Lord Jesus Christ taught us in **Mark 11:24 (TEV):**

"For this reason, I tell you: When you pray and ask for something, believe that you have received it, and you will be given whatever you ask for."

Help is always a prayer away, for we pray and believe that we have received, to have. When we face the challenges of love, we go to God and pray: "O LORD my God, give me the strength to love; give me the courage to persevere; give me the strength to forgive." We pause to add: 'Now I have the strength to love; now I have the courage to persevere; now I have the strength to forgive, in Jesus name, Amen.'" The walk of faith can be that simple, and the reality of the experience follows surprisingly.

The reason behind the answer to a prayer of faith is in **Hebrews 11:6 (TEV):**
"No one can please God without faith, for whoever comes to God must have faith that God exists and rewards those who seek him."

We must try not to trust in our will power to sustain our love at all times. Harsh realities can easily overrun such confidence. The Prophet Isaiah gave us the secret to great inner strength in **Isaiah 40:28-31 (NKJV):**

"Have you not known? Have you not heard? The everlasting God, the LORD, The Creator of the ends of the earth, neither faints nor is weary. His understanding is unsearchable.
"He gives power to the weak, And to those who have no might, He increases strength.

"Even the youths shall faint and be weary, And the young men shall utterly fall,

"But those who wait on the LORD Shall renew their strength; They shall mount up with wings like eagles, They shall run and not be weary, They shall walk and not faint."

CHAPTER TEN

THE VERTICAL LOVE

———— ◆◇◆ ————

4 "Hear, O Israel: The LORD our God, the LORD is one! 5 You shall love the LORD your God with all your heart, with all your soul, and with all your strength.

Deuteronomy 6:4-5 (NKJV)

We will need to take a close look at the place of love for our God in modulating various aspects of our horizontal love between a man and his wife. Our Lord Jesus Christ put love for God as the primary love that drives our horizontal love for our fellow men and women. Both Matthew and Mark recorded the incident. Here is the version in Mark's Gospel: **Mark 12:28-34 (NKJV):**

"Then one of the scribes came, and having heard them reasoning together, perceiving that He had answered them well, asked Him, "Which is the first commandment of all?"

"Jesus answered him, "The first of all the commandments is: **'Hear, O Israel, the LORD our God, the LORD is one.**

"And you shall love the LORD your God with all your heart, with all your soul, with all your mind, and with all your strength.' *This is the first commandment.*

"And the second, like it, is this: **'You shall love your neighbor as yourself.'** *There is no other commandment greater than these." (Bold emphasis mine)*

"So, the scribe said to Him, "Well said, Teacher. You have spoken the truth, for there is one God, and there is no other but He.

"And to love Him with all the heart, with all the understanding, with all the soul, and with all the strength, and to love one's neighbor as oneself, is more than all the whole burnt offerings and sacrifices."

"Now when Jesus saw that he answered wisely, He said to him, "You are not far from the kingdom of God." But after that, no one dared question Him."

The question was: "Which is the first commandment of all?" Our Lord Jesus Christ reached back to the Book of **Deuteronomy 6:4-5 (NKJV)**:

[4]*"Hear, O Israel: The LORD our God, the LORD is one!* [5]*You shall love the LORD your God with all your heart, with all your soul, and with all your strength."*

The Primary Love

The primary love is love for God. It is defining and controlling love. We need to understand the love for God and the control it exerts on our love so we can flourish in our love for others.

Loving God is Our Response

This truth is what the Bible teaches us - That we love God because He first loved us. **1 John 4:9-11 (NKJV)**

"In this, the love of God was manifested toward us, that God has sent His only begotten Son into the world, that we might live through Him. In this is love, not that we loved God, but that He loved us and sent His Son to be the propitiation for our sins. Beloved, if God so loved us, we also ought to love one another."

We learn that God's greatest act of love for all humanity is the sending of our Lord and Saviour Jesus Christ to come and die for our sins. We learn that God takes the initiative in love and His love inspires us to love Him in return. Not only that, but His love also encourages us to show love to one another.

Loving God is Transforming

When we come to see how much God loves us and how much His love cares and provides for us, we grow to become dependent on His love and learn to be deeply grateful for it. God's love changes us through the revelation of His care, provision, and protection. Our numerous testimonies of His guidance in key decisions and how His wisdom has saved us from many troubles reveal our dependence on God's love. We learn to be grateful for all that He is for us and all that He does to empower and provide for us. This gratitude becomes compelling gratitude, which the Apostle Paul describes in **2 Corinthians 5:14-15 (NKJV):**

¹⁴For the love of Christ compels us, because we judge thus: that if One died for all, then all died; ¹⁵and He died for all, that those who live should live no longer for themselves, but for Him who died for them and rose again.

God's greatest gift of love to me is Christ Jesus. The love of Christ drove Him to Calvary's Cross to die for my sins to reconcile God and me, and so make me one with God through His life. As a result of this special sustaining relationship, I am constrained to live the life of Christ and love like Him in the world.

So, when the Bible says in **Ephesians 5:21 (TEV):**
"Submit yourselves to one another because of your reverence for Christ;" We see that it is speaking of a love to which we can

never say no to or refuse to obey. Out of reverence for Christ is to make a demand of us we cannot refuse. A simple illustration will suffice.

Mr. Johnson is the elder brother of Peter's father. Peter was brilliant at school, but his father had no money to sponsor his education. Mr. Johnson was wealthy and had sent his children off to the best schools in the UK. Peter's father approached Mr. Johnson, and he took up Peter's education and sponsored him through school, both secondary and university. Peter came out of college, landed a great job in a multinational company, and became affluent. He left after a while to start his own company, which quickly flourished.

One day a scruffy looking young man came looking for him in his new office. He brought a letter from Mr. Johnson now retired to the village to rest. The note simply read: *"Please help me find a job for this young man. He has a promising future."* Without hesitation, the young man got an interview and a placement in his company. Said Peter afterward to his HR manager: "He came from my sponsor. He deserves an interview."

This story illustrates how the love of Christ compels us. When we remember what He went through for us, when we recall the quality and depth of His love and sacrifice, we accept to do for others something in the pattern of what He did for us.

Vertical love is controlling love. It is a compelling love. It compels, not by coercion but by the power of its love and care. It drives us with its depth of selflessness and sacrifice. The moment His love confronts us, it subdues us, and we submit to do as He bids us. But more on this later.

CHAPTER ELEVEN

THE BIBLE IS THE SOURCE OF
TRUTH AND VIRTUE

16 All Scripture is inspired by God and is useful for teaching the truth, rebuking error, correcting faults, and giving instruction for right living, 17 so that the person who serves God may be fully qualified and equipped to do every kind of good deed.

2 Timothy 3:16-17 (TEV)

When we marry Christians, it is presumed that the couple will accept the Bible's authority over their lives. This authority is a fundamental question we must resolve before we begin the union; we must abide by the teachings of the Word of God. Our task will be to be sure we understand what the Word of God is saying in every area of our lives. We must then add what we have understood to our lives so that love, peace, friendship, and harmony may reign in our home.

It is important to note that love, peace, friendship, and harmony is not a wish list. These are products of obedience to the truth, as revealed in the Word of God.

I was there when a man was asked why he was not joining his relations to look for wealth and riches by all means: his answer has stayed with me since I heard it some 49 plus years ago. Said the man, "The Bible has tied my hands." A Christian couple should have the same testimony to the world around them who want to know why they are not quarreling, shouting, and abusing each other as others. Their answer should be: "The Bible has tied our hands to love and virtue."

The Bible is given to us to teach us the truth that liberates and sets free, which we do not know; for rebuking error, correcting faults, and instruction in right living. Therefore, each couple must make every effort to study the Bible together. They must pray to model their life together on the solid foundation of the Word of God.

The Family Altar

This prayer time is an interactive session where they spend time reading and studying together, allowing the Holy Spirit to teach them the truth about God, their life together and other relationships with in-laws and friends. By studying God's Word, we dispel all our prejudices picked up here, there, and yonder as we were growing up. These prejudices include hostility against in-laws with or without cause. A Scripture that helps with this could be **Hebrews 13:1-2 (TEV):**

""Keep on loving one another as Christians.
"Remember to welcome strangers in your homes. There were some who did that and welcomed angels without knowing it." "

Warm hospitality melts hearts and eliminates many evils that arise from presumed hostilities and prejudices. As we meditate on the Word of God and pray together, the Holy Spirit teaches us to love and to conquer people through love.

Besides, the Word of God is the foundation of faith. Faith is the power in our souls that position us to trust God for great things as He unfolds the vision of our lives to us. Faith comes by hearing of the Word of God (Romans 10:17).

We renew our minds from misconceptions and prejudices with the Word of God (Romans 12:2). It is possible to have grown up or lived and worked in an environment where corruption is a way of life. As a result of personal pressure, we may not have resolved the matter of ethics and integrity of conduct for our lives, particularly in the marketplace. It may not be that we do not know the truth; the problem is that we pay lip-service to it. When we begin to study as a family, we realize that some of the positions we had taken hitherto are untenable. Through the study of God's Word, we embrace and imbibe necessary changes for the faith and spiritual health of the family.

There is a benefit that inspires the study of God's Word in **2 Peter 1:3-4 (NKJV:)**

"as His divine power has given to us all things that pertain to life and godliness, through the knowledge of Him who called us by glory and virtue, "by which have been given to us exceedingly great and precious promises, that through these you may be partakers of the divine nature, having escaped the corruption that is in the world through lust."

First, we need to become familiar with all the things given to us that relate to life and godliness. These come to us through the knowledge of Christ our Saviour.

Secondly, we need to progressively imbibe and experience all the beautiful promises that impart the divine nature into us. Besides, these promises also empower us to escape the corruption that is in the world through lust or inordinate desires.

The family altar will become even more essential when the couple begins to raise their own family. This prayer session is when they must make every effort to show the children that their parents try their best to live what they preach; they communicate their trust in the LORD God Almighty for who they are and thank Him for all their successes and achievements. They acknowledge Him as their strength and hope in difficult times. Children often get their greatest inspiration at the family altar, where they learn the truth about God and His Word from their parents. Parents need to model Christ-centred living for their children through precept and conduct. You teach it at the family altar: And you live it in your interactions in the family. I recall how I learned a lot of great Bible themes at the family altar, growing up at home. Many of those encounters helped shape me in those early days, even though my understanding of the truths were poor. But they left their mark in my heart.

CHAPTER TWELVE

THE RENEWED MIND

———————— ◆◇◆ ————————

Stop being conformed to this world, but continue to be transformed by the renewing of your minds so that you may be able to determine what is God's will – what is proper, pleasing, and perfect.

Romans 12:2 (ISV)

A Christian couple must have their mind renewed from the way the world thinks to what the Word of God teaches. For this reason, you don't copy what you see others doing, but instead, you seek to discover what the will of God is and what He expects us to do in every situation.

In this respect, we learn quite a few good things from our mentors and those who inspired us to lead godly lives. There is a story my father told me of his experience. His father had passed away by the time he was getting married. He had met my mother while he was conducting Sunday School classes in her village as a student of St. Paul's Teacher's College in Awka in Anambra state here in Nigeria. It was a sixty-mile journey or thereabouts from our town to that of my mother. After their wedding, his relations noted that each time men would sit down and talk, my mother would sit down and join in the conversation. One day, his family relations called him aside to say that it is not proper for a woman to sit down and join the men in their conversation. I could not forget how he said he responded to them. Said my father: "This is my house. My wife can sit down and talk with men. When we come to your house, and you want your wife to be deaf and dumb where men are, then that is ok for you." With that simple anecdote, my father taught me that a man is the head of his house and must not allow outsiders, no matter how well-meaning, to impose their values and ways on him as a Christian.

When it comes to the relationship between a man and his wife, there is no opinion shortage. As Christians, however, we must have our minds renewed no matter our cultural background to prove God's good, acceptable, and perfect will. It is not that we do not take counsel from friends and family. But whatever they say must find support in the Word of God and love.

The couple must travel this route of mind renewal together. They need each other's support to learn together and grow together. One helpful thing is never to argue with or reject truth in the Bible for whatever reason. This attitude is a secure foundation for the family always. Each family member learns to submit to the authority of the Word of God and to renew their minds and values to fall in line with the Word of God.

CHAPTER THIRTEEN

THE CRUCIFIED LIFE

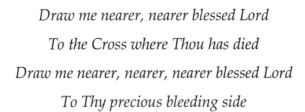

Draw me nearer, nearer blessed Lord

To the Cross where Thou has died

Draw me nearer, nearer, nearer blessed Lord

To Thy precious bleeding side

W̲e need the understanding of the crucified life to be comfortable with all the demands of spiritual life particularly within marriage. The crucified life is well-articulated by the Apostle Paul in **Galatians 2:20 (NKJV):**

²⁰ *I have been crucified with Christ; it is no longer I who live, but Christ lives in me; and the life which I now live in the flesh I live by faith in the Son of God, who loved me and gave Himself for me.*

When we are dead to self or our preferences and our needs, we are free from all carnal and self-centered constraints that make obedience to God and His Word difficult. The crucified life can be a tough call, but it is the only path that makes godliness in all things easy. It is the way to recreate the nature of Christ in us. It subjugates self-will under the will of God on earth. It is a nature that will be obedient to God and His Word. It is a nature that will showcase the virtue and power of the Kingdom of God in the life of a man on earth. When we are crucified with Christ, we are dead to self and all its desires but alive to God and His demands on us. What God demands of us produces the Christ-life in us, which manifests the Fruit of the Spirit as occasions demand.

Dead to Self - What does this mean?

This crucifixion creates a mind following hard after God to determine and do His will on earth as it is done in heaven. It derives from a studied appreciation of God's goodness and His loving kindness to us His people.

Psalm 63:1-8 (AMP)

1O GOD, You are my God, earnestly will I seek You; my inner self thirsts for You, my flesh longs and is faint for You, in a dry and weary land where no water is.

²So I have looked upon You in the sanctuary to see Your power and Your glory.

³Because Your loving-kindness is better than life, my lips shall praise You.

⁴ So will I bless You while I live; I will lift up my hands in Your name.

⁵My whole being shall be satisfied as with marrow and fatness; and my mouth shall praise You with joyful lips

⁶When I remember You upon my bed and meditate on You in the night watches.

⁷For You have been my help, and in the shadow of Your wings will I rejoice.

⁸ My whole being follows hard after You and clings closely to You; Your right hand upholds me.

When we follow hard after our God, we are driven by a passionate desire to walk this earth like our Lord Jesus who said in **John 5:19-20 (ISV):**

¹⁹ ... "Truly, truly I tell you, the Son can do nothing on His own accord, but only what He sees the Father doing. For what He does, the Son does likewise. ²⁰ For the Father loves the Son and shows Him everything He is doing. And He will show Him even greater works than these, so that you may be amazed.

As the Son does only what He sees the Father do, it is clear that the Son has dropped His will and desires to do the Father's will only. This life is the kind of life we live when we become crucified with Christ.

The crucified life is the shortest route to peace and harmony in the home. If the couple agrees to live this way, doing from the heart as our Lord Jesus would do in the situation, they will produce a relationship that has more joy and laughter than could be possible for them otherwise. It is not often that husband and wife are crucified at the same time. What tends to happen is that the more sanctified and godly of the two, will spearhead the change by talking and acting crucified. It may look as if they are paying too heavy a price for peace and harmony in the home on the surface. But two things come out of that. The first is that the Spirit of God will be with the obedient person driving through death to self, to evolve a life of love, peace, and harmony in the home.

Ideally, because the man is the head of the home, he should lead the way in demonstrating and manifesting the crucified life in the house. Where there is no movement from the man, the more sanctified and consecrated of the two parties should rise to lead the way. The crucified life empowers us to show love through humility and care despite any provocation in the home. We must remember that this obedience drives the flow of anointing, wisdom and the divine presence to the obedient person's side. We learn a great deal from the encounter of Joshua with the Commander of the Armies of the Living God in **Joshua 5:13-15 (NKJV):**

"And it came to pass, when Joshua was by Jericho, that he lifted his eyes and looked, and behold, a Man stood opposite him with His sword drawn in His hand. And Joshua went to Him and said to Him, "Are You for us or for our adversaries?"

"So He said, "No, but as Commander of the army of the LORD I have now come." And Joshua fell on his face to the earth and worshiped, and said to Him, "What does my Lord say to His servant?"

"Then the Commander of the LORD'S army said to Joshua, "Take your sandal off your foot, for the place where you stand is holy." And Joshua did so."

Joshua encounters a Man of War and boldly approaches Him to find out on whose behalf He has come to fight. The response he got was intriguing. *"I am neither for you nor your adversaries. I am here to see to the fulfillment of the purposes of the God of all heaven and earth."* Very revealing indeed! When a couple decides to live in obedience to God and His Word, the Commander is on their side, or more appropriately, they have chosen to be on the same side with the Commander. If only one of them is bending over to do what God wants in the relationship, then the Commander is with the obedient. Ever since I noticed the significance of this Scripture in the relationship between man and God, I realized that one way we can get God on our side is through obedience.

Dealing with Pride, Ego, and Insecurity

The crucified life deals a death blow to all decisions based on self-pride and ego. It discards all considerations of status, birth, wealth, and education to embrace the life of Christ revealed in **Philippians 2:5-11 (AMP):**

5Let this same attitude and purpose and [humble] mind be in you which was in Christ Jesus: [Let Him be your example in humility:]

6Who, although being essentially one with God and in the form of God [possessing the fullness of the attributes which make God God], did not think this equality with God was a thing to be eagerly grasped or retained,

7But stripped Himself [of all privileges and rightful dignity], so as to assume the guise of a servant (slave), in that He became like men and was born a human being.

8And after He had appeared in human form, He abased and humbled Himself [still further] and carried His obedience to the extreme of death, even the death of the cross!

9Therefore [because He stooped so low] God has highly exulted Him and has freely bestowed on Him the name that is above every name,

¹⁰That in (at) the name of Jesus every knee should (must) bow, in heaven and on earth and under the earth,
¹¹And every tongue [frankly and openly] confess and acknowledge that Jesus Christ is Lord, to the glory of God the Father.

The mind of Christ is humility. It attracts much favor from God. Pride is so destructive of marriage relationships that it makes two people compete rather than cooperate for the glory of God in their family unit. Pride is like a prism that distorts every thought and notion and makes sane communication and cooperation impossible. Alongside pride is the feeling of insecurity, which has another prism that distorts conversation and ideas. Insecurity is just as destructive of amity and friendship as pride.

On the other hand, humility is one way to gain entrance into the favor and blessings of God. It allows us to receive suggestions and ideas without distortion. The Scriptures repeatedly say that God resists the proud but gives grace to the humble (James 4:6; 1 Peter 5:5). Our Lord Jesus pointed the path to amity and friendship when He invited us to come and understudy His meekness: **Matthew 11:28-29 (NKJV):**
²⁸Come to Me, all you who labor and are heavily laden, and I will give you rest.

29Take My yoke upon you and learn from Me, for I am gentle and lowly in heart, and you will find rest for your souls.

We must state that those who do not understand a life of humility before God and man cannot show love like our Lord Jesus Christ, who is our model in all things. We serve through humility, and those who love serve those they love. He revealed this to his disciples to curb carnal ambitions in **Matthew 20:25-28 (NRSV):**

25But Jesus called them to him and said, "You know that the rulers of the Gentiles lord it over them, and their great ones are tyrants over them.

26 It will not be so among you, but whoever wishes to be great among you must be your servant,

27 and whoever wishes to be first among you must be your slave;

28 just as the Son of Man came not to be served but to serve, and to give his life a ransom for many."

Consider these anomalies: A situation where the man helps other women outside the home and in Church and is known as a gentleman to them but does not lift a finger to help his wife at home! The converse can be equally true: the woman is known for her humility and service outside the house and in Church but does not serve her husband at home. This type of scenario is why we can say that any virtue we have as Christians, which the people in our homes cannot testify to, does not exist. It may exist just for display and to impress outsiders. It is not true virtue. Our Lord Jesus demonstrated His virtues to His disciples and as the adage goes: "Charity begins at home."

Battling with Brokenness

When a man or woman has a broken spirit before the Lord, they have acquired that beatitude called 'poverty of the spirit.' This poverty of the spirit provides the disposition that embraces the rule and authority of the Kingdom of God in our lives and relationships. *"Blessed are the poor in spirit, for theirs is the Kingdom of heaven."* The poverty of the spirit is the hallmark of those who know that nothing they are and nothing they have can commend them before God. Instead, they have found their true worth in accepting the grace of God revealed in Christ Jesus, our Lord, and Saviour. We can build a strong and beautiful relationship through this spirit of brokenness, where we show love without hypocrisy and self-sacrifice is made with joy.

Do you love Me more than these?

This question will continue to haunt the saint who has not prioritized loyalty to God and His Christ above every other consideration. Peter went back to fishing after the death and resurrection of our Lord Jesus Christ. Perhaps, without the Master to command the supply of resources they were used to in their last three years and a half with Him, it was tempting to return to the business they were doing before He called them to follow Him. This encounter by the Sea of Galilee reveals that our Lord Jesus Christ demands complete loyalty from us. **John 21:15-18 (PassionNTPsa):**

15 After they had breakfast, Jesus said to Peter, "Simon, son of John, do you burn with love for me more than these?" Peter answered, "Yes, Lord! You know that I have great affection for you!" "Then take care of my lambs," Jesus said.

16 Jesus repeated his question the second time, "Simon, son of John, do you burn with love for me?" Peter answered, "Yes, my Lord! You know that I have great affection for you!" "Then take care of my sheep," Jesus said.

17 Then Jesus asked him again, "Peter, son of John, do you have great affection for me?" Peter was saddened by being asked the third time and said, "My Lord, you know everything. You know that I burn with love for you!"

18 Peter, listen, when you were younger, you made your own choices, and you went where you pleased. But one day when you are old, others will tie you up and escort you where you would not choose to go – and you will spread out your arms."

The couple in Christ understands the idea of work and responsibility to provide for their family's needs. However, they know that in doing so, they must pursue righteousness and the will of God as those who will give account to God one day about how they lived their lives here on earth. Our Lord Jesus Christ confronted Peter with questions of priority and loyalty. The conversation in **Luke 22:31-34 (NKJV)** will suffice.

31 And the Lord said, "Simon, Simon! Indeed, Satan has asked for you, that he may sift you as wheat.
32 But I have prayed for you, that your faith should not fail; and when you have returned to Me, strengthen your brethren."
33 But he said to Him, "Lord, I am ready to go with You, both to prison and to death."
34 Then He said, "I tell you, Peter, the rooster shall not crow this day before you will deny three times that you know Me."

The Apostle Peter was the leader of the band of eleven disciples who were the sole custodians of the message of grace destined for humanity. To revert to fishing was to lose focus and to have misplaced priority. Thankfully they failed again as they had failed before, and thankfully too, they went straight back to their calling in Christ.

A young Christian couple working and praying on their future would need to steer their path in the direction of the will of God for their lives together. That is the only way to fulfill destiny with success in their chosen fields of endeavour.

CHAPTER FOURTEEN

BE STRONG IN THE LORD

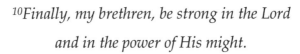

*¹⁰Finally, my brethren, be strong in the Lord
and in the power of His might.*
- Ephesians 6:10 (NKJV)

In concluding his extensive write-up on the new life in Christ for the Christian, the Apostle Paul noted that those who desire to live the Christian life in their families and society would need to be strong in the LORD and in the power of His might. What follows this assertion is details of our struggle between light and darkness, good and evil, and between self and the will of God. He states quite categorically that in trying to live the Christian life the way we are taught, we should expect to fight off spiritual forces that would want to take us down and out from that straight and narrow way that leads to eternal life.

Strength to Love

We gain this strength by the infusion of spiritual energy into our human spirit by the Spirit of God. We learn about this from **Ephesians 3:14-16 (NKJV):**

14 For this reason I bow my knees to the Father of our Lord Jesus Christ, 15 from whom the whole family in heaven and earth is named, 16 that He would grant you, according to the riches of His glory, to be strengthened with might through His Spirit in the inner man.

With this energy infusion, we can allow the Holy Spirit to manifest the love of Christ through us, with humility, self-sacrifice, and service. These are the three things our Lord Jesus revealed when He washed the feet of His disciples.

Loving through Faith

It is essential to understand how this plays out. We access the infused spiritual energy by faith. The path is to allow our Lord Jesus to dwell in our hearts by faith so that we can be rooted and grounded in love through Him as the Bible says in **Ephesians 3:17-19 (NKJV):**

17 that Christ may dwell in your hearts through faith; that you, being rooted and grounded in love, 18 may be able to comprehend with all the saints what is the width and length and depth and height-- 19 to know the love of Christ which passes knowledge; that you may be filled with all the fullness of God.

When we face love challenges in our home, the Holy Spirit whispers what our love response should be. If we find the path challenging because of ego problems or serious misgivings, the Holy Spirit releases much grace to get us over the obstacles to respond the way we should rather than the way we think or feel. For example, suppose a man is starving, and the food is not ready; that may cause him to grumble and complain and criticize his wife. But the Holy Spirit may nudge him to find a snack for everybody and then go to see how he can help in the kitchen. This Spirit control is how love becomes an act of obedience out of reverence for the indwelling Christ. When we respond to our spouse as the Holy Spirit bids us, we love by faith with the Holy Spirit's inner resources. Those who continuously react positively to the Holy Spirit's constraints trade their self-centered responses for self-sacrificing love, humility, and service.

Be strong in the Lord.

The inner strength that the Holy Spirit gives empowers us to yield to His leadership and direction. "As many as are led by the

Spirit of the Lord are children of God" (Romans. 8:14). As we follow His leading and promptings, we can sense this inner strength that faith unveils in our responses. We begin to exhibit a capacity for love and service with humility beyond our natural inclination and ability.

There is also extensive mind renewal that follows this obedience. We can see why the Bible says that those who follow the Holy Spirit rather than their flesh or natural inclinations fulfill the law's righteous requirement (Romans 8:4). We change our thinking by following the Holy Spirit as He propels us to obey the Word of God. With time, these promptings and our obedience begin to manifest a character change that reveals the nature of Christ through us. Without fear of contradiction, I can say that this type of transformation in character is impossible without a functional dependence on the Holy Spirit. He makes it look simple and easy and yet profound and far-reaching in its implication.

The Prayer that brings Change

I learned concerning the challenge of following the teachings of the Bible in everything, that those who go to the LORD in prayer to say: *"LORD I want to do it, but I am seriously challenged: Please come and do it in me so that You can do it through me."* These are the people with the testimony of victory. One day, they wake up to discover that they have as it were, climbed up to a pedestal and can now look down at what was a vast mountain before. Now they can wonder out loud: "And what made it so, so challenging before?" The Spirit of God knows how to take us past an obstacle by taking us higher so we can look down with a bemused smile. The challenge may have been from background culture, habit, or other antecedents. But eureka! The Holy Spirit has taken us beyond all the constraints so we can experience and relish the joy of obedience to the LORD and His Word, known only to those who obey.

The Joy of the wonders of His grace

It is often a bemused reflection that draws that deep joy and the smile that paints the corners of our lips when we survey how far the grace of God has taken us. We went from that self-centered and crankiest pride that we started with to the mellowed, spiritually sensitive soul, eager to obey the LORD in our lives. It comes with deep satisfaction in the knowledge that the grace of God can propel us beyond our natural self to make a spiritual person out of us. We read the Scripture in Paul's first letter to the Corinthians with deeper interest. Two passages that are close together are of interest. The first is **1 Corinthians 2:14-16 (NKJV):**

14But the natural man does not receive the things of the Spirit of God, for they are foolishness to him; nor can he know them, because they are spiritually discerned.

15But he who is spiritual judges all things, yet he himself is rightly judged by no one.

*16 For "**who has known the mind of the LORD** that he may instruct Him?" But we have the mind of Christ.*

We look back and see when we were natural and how distinct it is from where we now are when the spiritual man seems quite natural to us. The Apostle indicted the Corinthian Church for still being natural and carnal long after they had come to Christ in **1 Corinthians 3:1-4 (NKJV):**

1And I, brethren, could not speak to you as to spiritual people but as to carnal, as to babes in Christ.

*2I fed you with milk and not with solid food; for until now you were not able to **receive** it, and even now you are still not able;*

3for you are still carnal. For where there are envy, strife, and divisions among you, are you not carnal and behaving like mere men?

4For when one says, "I am of Paul," and another, "I am of Apollos," are you not carnal?

When life in the spirit looks natural to us, we must thank and bless the Lord with all our hearts for the wonders of His grace. It has not always been so.

CHAPTER FIFTEEN

TO HAVE AND TO HOLD

———— ◆◇◆ ————

For if by the one man's offense death reigned through the one, much more those who receive abundance of grace and of the gift of righteousness will reign in life through the One, Jesus Christ.
Romans 5:17 (NKJV)

T he Bible tells us the two things we must receive to reign in life in this world. The first is the gift of righteousness through Christ, which brings us the salvation of our souls. This gift is by grace through faith, which has the power to clean up our lives and give us a fresh start. Whether newly-wed or long-married, a couple can enter into a new life when they receive or reaffirm the gift of righteousness they received in Christ and step forward to lead a new life by the abundant grace of God.

Taking Personal Responsibility

There is something that consolidates this resolve to have and to hold in love till death or rapture part you. It is when the individual takes personal responsibility for obedience to God and His Word in a marriage relationship. It is signaled by a commitment prayer that says: *"LORD, whatever may happen here in this marriage, I want You to count on me to obey and do what You command. All I ask for is the abundance of Your grace to take me through any and every challenge."*

What is this Abundance of Grace?

God's grace is made available to the sinner for salvation and to the redeemed for victorious Christian living. For these two objectives, we may split the grace of God into different parts for better understanding:

Saving Grace

The grace that brings salvation or **saving grace**. (Ephesians 2:8). Here is the version in **Titus 2:11-12 (NIV):**

11 For the grace of God that brings salvation has appeared to all men.
12 It teaches us to say "No" to ungodliness and worldly passions, and to live self-controlled, upright, and godly lives in this present age,

Sustaining Grace

There is the all-pervading grace and favour of God that keeps us from day to day as our *sustaining grace.* (**Luke 2:40 (NIV):** [40]*And the child grew and became strong; he was filled with wisdom, and the grace of God was upon him.*

Enabling Grace

There is the grace to help in times of need or the *enabling grace.* (**Hebrews 4:16 (NIV):** [16]*Let us then approach the throne of grace with confidence, so that we may receive mercy and find grace to help us in our time of need.)*

Quickening Grace

There is the grace that empowers us to do great things for God's glory or the *quickening grace:* (**Acts 4:33 (NIV)**

[33]*With great power the apostles continued to testify to the resurrection of the Lord Jesus, and much grace was upon them all.*

Empowering Grace

We also have the *empowering grace* that produces results that are way beyond expectation as was seen in Antioch. **Acts 11:21-23 (NIV):**

*21The Lord's hand was with them, and a great number of people believed and turned to the Lord. 22 News of this reached the ears of the church at Jerusalem, and they sent Barnabas to Antioch. 23 When he arrived and **saw the evidence of the grace of God**, he was glad and encouraged them all to remain true to the Lord with all their hearts. (1 Cor. 3:10) (Bold emphasis – mine.)*

Performing Grace

There is the **performing grace** given for the fulfillment of our calling in Christ. **Romans 1:5 (NIV):**

5Through him and for his name's sake, we received grace and apostleship to call people from among all the Gentiles to the obedience that comes from faith.

The Workings of Abundant Grace

8And God is able to make all grace abound toward you, that you, always having all sufficiency in all things, may have an abundance for every good work.

- 2 Corinthians 9:8 (NKJV)

This is the mystery of the workings of grace that is abundant. In all things and at all times, no matter what the situation calls for, we have capacity supplied through grace to drive the correct response that will lead to God's glory in our lives. Grace always works through faith to scale every mountain be it within us or outside. If humility is needed, there will be grace to bend low and bend over to meet the challenge. If self-sacrifice is needed, there will be grace to awaken to the need and do it with joy and without murmuring and complaining.

Grace begins with a silent prayer of faith at every challenge. The Holy Spirit honors the trust and infuses a willingness and ability to follow the path that will lead to the glory of God in our lives. The glory of God is the ultimate pursuit of man. No matter the place of our calling and no matter when and how the challenge presents, grace provides what we need to glorify God. For this reason, the Scripture says that those who have an abundance of grace reign in this life. They do not rely on their strength. They reach out through faith enabled by grace to overcome and reign in and over every situation.

I Love My Spouse

This declaration is a beautiful thing for a couple to say to each other. But if they were to add, "And I have abundant grace to love my spouse and to continue to love my spouse," then consistency is guaranteed no matter the challenge that surfaces. When the Apostle Paul declared in 1st Corinthians 15:10 that *"By the grace of God, I am what I am,"* he wanted all to know that grace is a sure foundation to build on without fear of failure." Everyone needs grace that is sufficient for every situation. To have enough grace, always is to be blessed and highly favored. It is great wisdom to rely always on the grace of God in our lives to build a healthy, warm, and affectionate relationship filled with love and laughter.

The Two Prayers

The Man: O LORD my God, please give me abundant grace to love my wife as Christ loved His Church and gave His life for her. Lord Jesus, I accept that it is love that must drive submission. So, help me love my wife and lead my family with a self-sacrificing love that we as a family will glorify God in our lives, in Jesus' name, Amen.

The Woman: O LORD my God, please give me abundant grace to submit to my husband out of love and out of reverence to Christ. I trust You to protect my obedience as You transform my husband and me to lead our family with transparency and self-sacrificing love that will cause us to glorify Your name in our lives, in Jesus' name, Amen.

CHAPTER SIXTEEN

THERE'S ROOM FOR EVERYONE

———————— ◆◇◆ ————————

A befitting closure to a book like this should centre on the understanding of love for all the family. We will revert to the Greeks and their four kinds of love: *Sturge, Phileo, Eros and Agape.*

There have been several efforts by many authors to help couples get along and be happy doing so. In a Christian marriage, the choice of a spouse is and should always be between the individual and his or her God. It is for that reason that I choose to begin with friendship.

To have and to hold until death or rapture parts you cannot just be with anybody. It must be for that somebody you believe you can share the rest of your life with, but how to know that somebody is not the subject of this book. For that, you will have to go to *You May Kiss the Bride* for details. This book assumes that you found a friend, fell in love and married. Now you are trying to live happily ever after.

Friendship Love

The Greeks will say through *phileo,* "Since you started off as friends, continue in the same vein and let your friendship deepen."

The friendship of a man and his wife has quite a few descriptions in the Bible that reveals its core value.

- There is the iron that sharpens iron. (Proverbs 27:17) I was told the story of a young man who went to his counsellor to complain that his fiancée was always correcting his spoken English when they are together. The counsellor told him that it was the best place to correct it. He told him it was better to correct it there than have him make such obvious mistakes in public. He was worried that it could be lack of respect. The counsellor agreed if only it happened in public. But it should be done privately to protect their public image. My father told the story of a white missionary lady that married a motor mechanic. She taught him to read and write so she could have him join her company as well. The friendship within a couple's relationship must be such as to tell each other the truth in love. If we are negative to such corrections it may mean that we are struggling with some form of insecurity. We were told in our elementary school days that no one is above correction.

- A spouse is the friend that sticks closer than a brother (Proverbs 18:24). Understandably because the two have become one and have many bonds that one cannot have with a sibling, the relationship between a man and his wife is much deeper than that between siblings. After a while, siblings can only come and go. A spouse is there for all seasons.

- Another hallmark of this friendship is trust and transparency. The problem with telling a lie, is that you lose the posture of a truth teller. A discovered lie ruins one's reputation. From the moment the lie is discovered, the question of credibility will always lurk in the background for quite a while.

- Suffice it to say that the deeper the warmth and affection shared, the simpler the relationship will run. The more transparent, the more trust there will be. And humility has this wonderful way of disarming quarrels. As our

Lord Jesus taught us, the meek and lowly in heart always find rest for their souls.

Conjugal Love – *eros*

Married couples nourish their love with *phileo and eros.* They use friendship to build a warm and affectionate relationship and use conjugal love to build soul ties. The Greek word for soul is *psuche,* which simply means life. When conjugal love is deeply satisfying on both sides, intangible bonds connect the two people and they are able to love and care sacrificially without grumbling and complaining.

Parental Love

This is both instinctive and studied. It is quite instinctive in the mother because of pregnancy and breastfeeding. For the man it is a studied love because he will need to learn to get involved in the life of the baby right from birth in order to bond with the child. Little chores like nappy change, bottle feeding of expressed breast milk and rocking a crying baby are ways that men can bond early with the children. That angry scowl that says, "Take this baby away, I want to sleep," should not be made at all." No father would want his child to grow up and hear that statement. It does not augur well for bonding.

Unconditional Love - *agapeo*

I believe that agape is a reserve love that we use if the going gets tough and rough and there is a great deal of hurt and pain. In a good relationship a man and his wife must have many reasons for loving and caring for each other. Through forgiveness and meekness, they have little need for the love that is a choice of the will because every other bond of friendship or soul tie has failed. *Agapeo* should always be there for God's obedient children so that we can will to love, to care and to forgive when all passion and bonds of friendship are gone. Agape has the capacity to rebuild and repair the other two loves and nourish them back to health again. It comes equipped with patience, humility and service.

Perhaps, St. Ignatius Loyola's prayer should also suffice for families who hold *agapeo* in reserve:

ST IGNATIUS LOYOLA (1491 - 1556)

Teach us, good Lord to serve thee as thou deservest,
  to give and not to count the cost;
  to fight and not to heed the wounds;
  to toil and not to seek for rest;
  to labour and not to ask for any reward;
  except that of knowing that we do thy will. **Amen.**

ABOUT THE AUTHOR

──────── ◆◇◆ ────────

D r. Okey Onuzo is a Consultant Nephrologist and Chief Medical Director of the first private dialysis hospital in Nigeria – The Life Support Medical Centre, which began the treatment of kidney patients in 1986. He qualified as a medical doctor from the University of Ibadan Medical School in 1976 and did his one year internship at the University College Hospital, Ibadan. He did his residency program at the Lagos University Teaching hospital and did his Fellowship in Nephrology at the Strong Memorial Hospital in Rochester New York. He got introduced to evangelical Christianity through the Scripture Union in 1970 and gave his life to Christ on June 28, 1970. He entered ministry through the Ibadan Varsity Christian Union and got called at an anointing service in 1973 to an Apostolic Ministry, with emphasis on teaching and the prophetic. He has worked and ministered with different organizations and was for over 30 years an associate Pastor of the National headquarters Church of the Foursquare

Gospel in Nigeria. He also worked with the Full Gospel Business Men's Fellowship where he was a pioneer chapter President and rose to be a National Director. On September 3rd, 2011, he was led to pioneer the Kingdom Life Seminar, a teaching and discipleship ministry with the vision of raising men and women who desire to walk daily in the footprints of our Lord Jesus Christ. He wrote and published his first book, Pathway to Conversational Prayer in 1988 and since then has written and published 9 other books. He is married to Mariam and they have four children and grandchildren.

BOOKS BY OKEY ONUZO

1. Pathway to Conversational Prayer
2. The Convert and the Counsellor
3. Dimensions of Faith
4. You May Kiss the Bride
5. God's Will the Way to Power
6. Minspi (A work of Fiction)
7. Prayer Relationship
8. The Beatitudes
9. Spiritual Intelligence
10. Between Love and Submission

Made in the USA
Middletown, DE
08 April 2021